Warrior Spirit Rising
A Native American Spiritual Journey

Dianna Good Sky

First paperback edition June 2020

Book design by Didi King at www.csjkingpublishing.com

Cover by Mark Lambertson at www.ProdigiousMotion.com

Cover photo and feather by Mel Goodsky

The great photo on the back cover was taken at Lake Vermillion Pow Wow by a photographer who gave me permission to use it, but whose email has long since been misplaced. I'm sorry, but thank you.

ISBN: 979-8-6527-2277-7

www.DiannaGoodSky.com

The events and conversations in this book have been set down to the best of the author's ability, although some names and details have been changed to protect the privacy of individuals.

DEDICATION

Thank you for letting me tell your story, dad. When I first asked you and you said no. I didn't like it. Then, under pressure from me years later, you explained to me that you would know when the time is right, and I didn't like it. Now, I understand. And I am so proud to be your daughter. *MiiGwetch* Dad.

For my favorite oldest son, Francis.
For my favorite youngest son, Curtis.
For my favorite oldest daughter, Nikole.
For my favorite youngest daughter, Katherine.
I dedicate this work to you. I made promises to you before you were even born and I will continue to be the best mom and grandma I can be. I love you all so much. For the last time, my children—equally.

To my little sister and brother, Lela and Curtis, who shared both the pain and the joy in this journey, I love you with all that is in me.

Lastly, this is for my beautiful mom, Arlene. Without whom I do not think I could have handled all the crazy. I love you, Mom.

CONTENTS

	Acknowledgments	i
	Introduction	ii
1	Ryan's Story	1
2	The Ancestors	8
3	Sugar Bush	15
4	Grandfather's Charcoal	23
5	Changes	27
6	Service to Country	38
7	Reservation and Relocation	42
8	U.S. Navy Seabee	49
9	Virginia	56
10	Payday	67
11	Losing Everything	72
12	Dream of the Light	80
13	Town Drunk	86
14	Death and Life	89
15	A Return to Home	99
16	The Gift of Medicine	105
17	Teacher	110
18	Healer	117
19	Spiritual Advisor	122
20	The Warrior	128
	Epilogue	137
	Author's Note	140

ACKNOWLEDGMENTS

This book would not have been possible without the help of my team who have become my friends. To say that I couldn't have done it alone is an understatement.

My editor, Chelsea—you held my hand through this process and the book is far better because of your guidance.

My photographer Mel—These photos! Your photography skills are out of this world. How you managed to capture all of my dad's soul in a photo is truly a remarkable skill. Then, when you sent me the photo of the feather with the red, I knew it was perfect for the book. Much love sister.

My design artist Mark—I knew you would be able to convey my dad's story through your cover design when I saw your first draft. I couldn't love it more.

What do I call you Didi and Jeff King? Your skill and brilliance in the proofreading, typesetting, and help with the self-publishing was far beyond my expectations and I couldn't be more grateful for your help and your knowledge.

Steve—I appreciate your feedback and assistance with this book but also your encouragement for me to actually write. You were the first to tell me I should write a book, and even though this story isn't what neither of us expected to be the first, I promise, Blue Eyed Chippewa is coming.

For all my friends, especially my sister U.S. Navy Chiefs. Your love and support throughout the process and your patience have been so heartwarming to me. You held me up when I needed it and I will be forever grateful that I am surrounded by such beautiful people and belong to such a beautiful organization.

Russ and Ryan Holman: I cannot thank you enough for your friendship with my dad and for sharing your story.

I am grateful for the Richardson family, for always being kind to my family.

These people have been such an important part of my family's life, and I wanted to take a moment to give them a little extra shout out.

Ryan Holman: http://rusticrailings.com/

Richardson's Shangri-la Resort: http://www.rs-l.com/

They have excellent customer service (because they are great people) and if you end up doing business with them, tell them you read about them in **Warrior Spirit Rising.**

INTRODUCTION

When I left for boot camp in January of 1980, my father was a drunk. I don't even remember if he saw me off. What I do remember is the day I told him I was joining the Navy.

I was on my way home from the movies with friends when I stopped at a bar to use the bathroom since we were still twenty miles from the Bois Forte Reservation where my family lived. This bar, Glendale, was the last stop on Highway 53, before the Reservation road turn.

I saw him the moment I walked through the door—my dad, the town drunk. One of them, anyway. Quietly, I made my way toward the bathroom, hoping he wouldn't see me. Despite my attempt at hiding from him, the familiar tones of his voice carried across the bar as he called out to me: "Hey, babe." There was no avoiding an encounter. I had to stop and talk to him. *Shit*.

My dad spent fourteen years in the Navy, and I had spent most of my life away from the Reservation, traveling with him from base to base. I knew, or at least I thought I knew, that my recent decision to sign the papers and join up would make him proud.

So, I begrudgingly walked over to where he sat on the barstool and decided to share my news.

"You're going to join the Navy?" he said in disbelief. "I mean, only dikes and whores join the Navy." He paused. "For girls anyway."

I blushed, then lifted my head in slight defiance. "Well, I'm not either one of those," I said.

"I know, babe."

I stood awkwardly next to him, wishing I didn't have to be there, regretting my decision to stop and use the bathroom. I should have just gone to the bathroom on the dark twenty-mile stretch of highway between here and the Rez. If I had done that, at least I wouldn't be standing here right now. The dim room smelled like cheap beer and body odor, and the droning music in the background barely overpowered the buzz of neon signs and drunken conversations.

"You know what, babe?" he finally said. "If you join the Navy…I'll sober up."

I looked at him for a bit, and with my voice sounding somewhere between a third grader and the eighteen-year-old that I was, I said, "Really Dad?"

He took another drink of his Pabst Blue Ribbon beer. "Yep. I will."

I began to wonder just how many times he'd said that before. And I didn't know what to say to him.

I had watched alcohol ruin my parents' marriage. Ruin our relationship. The Reservation was a living testimony of the damage that alcoholism can inflict on the world. Before alcohol took hold of my dad, we were a normal family with an almost storybook existence. We played catch in the backyard, we watched TV together and played games as a family. Dad would cook breakfast every Sunday—his day to cook—and my mom would always have dinner waiting for him, every evening.

And then everything changed. Instead of waiting for him each night with dinner on the table, we sat waiting with empty cupboards, hoping he would come home with money so we could buy groceries. He stopped playing with us and we stopped expecting anything from him.

Standing in the bar, next to my inebriated father, I weighed the facts. Of course, I wanted my dad back. The thought of him sobering up if I joined the Navy was incredible. I was hopeful. For a moment. I also remembered the many times that he went to treatment, only to come back home and start drinking again.

The small hope I felt dissipated as quickly as it had come. Without another word, I hugged my dad, gently kissed his stinky cheek, and walked out of the bar.

As we drove the last twenty miles home, I stared out the window while my friends chattered about who knows what. I thought about what my dad had said in the bar. What if he does it? What if my dad really does get sober? The thought thrilled me, but I knew it was wishful thinking.

After that night, I pushed it out of my mind. I left for boot camp shortly after and threw myself into my new career. The first eight weeks of basic training were all-consuming, and we were allowed very few interactions with the outside world. When I was finally allowed a phone call, I dialed my mom—I didn't even know how to get a hold of my dad.

Mom is who I relied upon for everything anyways. My parents had divorced many years earlier, but my mom still kept tabs on Dad from time to time. They both lived on the Bois Forte Reservation—it was hard to avoid each other, even if they wanted to.

Over the phone, she told me that after I left for the Navy, Dad had checked himself into a treatment center. I was floored. My dad had actually followed through on his promise. I was surprised he even remembered making it. There I was at Navy boot camp, holding the phone in my hand, and I was absolutely hopeful—and absolutely scared. Or maybe it was more like a preemptive fear that I, no, our whole family, would be disappointed—again.

After boot camp, I went through Apprentice ("A") school for Oceanographic Systems Technician before I was allowed a visit home. I had received my first orders to go overseas, and I took the opportunity to be with my family before heading out of the country. Once back on the Reservation, I was very surprised to learn that my dad was still sober. At that point, it was the longest he had been sober by about six or seven months.

When I finally saw him, I was shocked. Just months earlier, when I left home, my dad had short, black hair with maybe a smattering of gray here and there. Now, his hair hung down to his shoulders, as white as the moon. I wasn't sure who this man was standing in front of me.

My dad began to share a story with me, the story of how his life changed. At first, while he spoke, I began to wonder if he had just replaced alcohol with marijuana. He sounded high, or at least delusional. The things he shared with me were far-fetched. He spoke of a near-death experience, an encounter so far outside of the realm of possibility. *Who is this man?* I thought, not for the first time.

Then, just as I was wondering what to make of his tale, he said, "You know, in Alcoholics Anonymous they tell us that we're not supposed to say that we're never going to take another drink again."

He looked me dead in the eye as he made his next statement. "But I know that I will never drink again."

As our eyes met, I knew. I knew, at that moment, that his declaration was true.

My dad is sober to this day. I didn't believe his story at the time, but I did believe in him.

It has been forty years since my dad went from the town drunk to a spiritual advisor, teacher, and healer. This is the story of my dad, Gene Goodsky—how he lived, how he almost died, and how he came back a different man. And how he went on to positively impact the world of all those around him, starting with himself.

1
RYAN'S STORY
1994

I t was the winter of 1994 when Ryan Holman was in a terrible accident.

Ryan was with his friends, visiting a cabin outside of Cook, MN. They were there to hang out and enjoy the beautiful snow packed outdoors. The kids, most of them recent high school graduates, set off to drive on the snowmobile trails. The area was secluded, with plenty of snow-capped trees, yet had a smattering of homes with large open fields full of the white powder that made the snowmobiles glide across with speed and ease. They could stick to trails or make their own. Most of them chose to do both.

Ryan was maneuvering smoothly right along with the rest of the boys. But none of them noticed the chain that lay across the driveway on this particular path. He was driving his snowmobile when everything went wrong, and the world turned upside down. Before anyone knew what happened, Ryan was pinned to the back of his snowmobile, the chain cutting across his chest. He said he was fine, but they knew he wasn't. Instead of standing around and arguing, they rushed Ryan's damaged body to the small community hospital in Cook.

The chain had cut the main artery from Ryan's heart to his liver, and seventy percent of his liver was smashed. In Cook, they did their best to treat him, but really, this was too big of an accident for them to handle, and his blood pressure kept dropping. Instead, they life-flighted him to Duluth, where he might have a better chance. It was a bigger hospital and it was much more equipped for this type of accident.

The accident turned out to be so much more serious than anyone, especially Ryan, thought it was. For months, the Duluth hospital became a second home for the Holmans.

After five surgeries, the eighteen-year-old had lost over fifty pounds. His chest had been stitched, buttoned and zipped, and still the wound wouldn't heal. Ryan spent two months in Duluth before he was finally stable enough to be sent home. Two weeks later, however, the infection had returned to his chest and he was back in the hospital.

The Goodskys and the Holmans go back at least a generation or two. The Holman family lived in Orr, the town nearest the Goodsky allotment. Russell Holman, Ryan's father, is a Scandinavian Christian with blond hair and blue eyes. Gene Goodsky is a full-blooded Indian with dark skin and equally dark features. Despite the difference in their backgrounds and upbringing, the two men had solidified their friendship many years before.

Dad and Russ had attended school together in Orr. Years later, Dad worked for Russell's log cabin business, helping to build homes. And Russ, like Dad, had been a Seabee in the Navy. They even ran into each other one time in Gulfport, Mississippi in 1968 at Seabee Boot Camp. But that was a long time ago and a long way from Orr.

Dianna Good Sky

The city of Orr (I get a kick out of the fact that it's called a city, with its population of about 300), sits right on Highway 53, which extends into Canada, just forty miles to the north. Orr also sits on Pelican Lake, a six-mile stretch of Minnesota beauty, filled with giant bluegills and crappies.

The lakeshore runs along the west side of town, while the railroad line runs along the east and through the town itself. The railroad track divides the town. The gas station, post office, general store, Pattenn's Café, and the liquor store, now affectionately called The Muni, sit on one side.

Across the tracks are the Orr school building, laundromat, and housing. Orr School once held classes in grades one through six for students from the area, excluding the Indians from the nearest Reservation. The Reservation Indians didn't attend Orr School until seventh grade when they were bussed the twenty miles into town. But there were Indian allotments much closer to Orr, and all the Indians who lived there, including Dad, attended Orr School from day one.

It was those Indians (mostly Goodskys) that took the brunt of the racism that was prevalent in the area. Because they lived off the Reservation and spent most of their lives near Orr, they encompassed just a small representation of the Indians in northern Minnesota. Their involvement in sports, however, proved to the white kids that the Indians had something to offer Orr School. By the time the Reservation kids arrived at Orr School in the seventh grade, the other Indians from the area had developed good relationships with the white kids. Most of them, anyway.

Dad learned about Ryan's accident not long after it happened. Orr was a small town and it was a major accident: word traveled quickly. But it was a few months after the accident, while in town, that Dad ran into Ryan's parents.

"How's the boy?" He asked them. His concern was apparent. He and Ryan had worked together at Russell's business and Dad always thought very highly of the boy. With obvious concern, Russ told my Dad that it was not good. He had been, at that point, nearly three months in the hospital, and the doctors said there was nothing else they could do. They had sent Ryan home again, this time for good.

Dad knew he could help if they let him.

The locals called my dad the "medicine man," but he wasn't really *Mide*, or in any way associated with the *Midewiwin*, the medicine society. They knew he was the Spiritual Advisor for the Bois Forte Band of Chippewa, and they also knew that Gene was their friend. Not sure what else to do for their son, the Holmans agreed to have Dad come to the house. His instructions were fairly simple: have tobacco ready for an offering. The Holmans were Christian, and they understood that they were inviting Gene Goodsky to their home for more than just good thoughts and a quick prayer.

Ryan was dying and he knew it. The wound on his chest was now green, and he could feel the endless tugging at his soul and body that could only be one thing: death. When he tried to fight it, the pain would shoot through his body. When he gave himself over to die, the pain would leave. He felt numb. He felt nothing. And he was so very tired. He wanted it to end. He was ready to give over to the peace that he hoped death would bring.

He was lying on the couch in his parents' living room when Dad arrived. Ryan couldn't move and could barely comprehend what was happening, but he recognized Dad's face and was glad to see him. Besides their time spent working in the summer, Dad taught cultural studies at several of the area schools, including the high school that Ryan had attended. But Ryan also remembered that Gene had been a Seabee too, just like his father. That comforted him as he understood why his own father trusted my dad.

Dianna Good Sky

The tobacco stood in a dish in the living room when Dad arrived at the Holman's home. Russell and his wife, Veronica, greeted him warmly, but Dad could see the worry on their faces. If you have ever watched your children suffer, you understand, and Ryan was not doing well.

Dad took one look at Ryan and wasted no time in beginning his ceremony. He accepted their tobacco and held it in his hand. He brought out a jug of tea that he had brewed specifically for Ryan. When he learned what was happening with Ryan's wound, he had collected a selection of local plants and herbs and made the tea just as he had been taught by the elders.

Dad then offered up the tobacco to the Spirits, pulled out his pipe, and began smoking—as was tradition. The Holmans watched with slight apprehension as Dad started praying in Anishinaabemowin. He prayed and smoked, and they began to relax, feeling curiously comforted by Dad's voice and words, even though they had no idea what he was saying.

Toward the end of his ceremony, or prayer, Dad gently set a leather beaded rosette—with a beaded turtle as the centerpiece— on Ryan's chest, just above the festering wound. Immediately and for the first time since he had arrived, Ryan lifted his head. He lifted it with a jolt and much more energy and strength than he had felt for a long time.

"Holy shit!" he said. His parents, startled, looked from Ryan to Dad. "I'm sorry," Ryan mumbled, looking at his mother. Dad motioned for him to "shhh." Ryan tried to relax back into the couch.

Ryan's parents were almost as shocked to see their weak son lift his head so far upright as they were to hear him curse in front of his mom. But that didn't matter at the moment. They knew something had just happened to their son. They were "cautiously optimistic and hopeful," as Russell told me later.

After Ryan finished drinking about a pint of this tea through his straw, Dad finally finished his ceremony. He then asked Ryan if he was okay. Ryan told him "When I took that first drink through the straw, I started to feel like something was pulling something out of my wound. And it's hot. I feel hot all over."

It was hard for Ryan to drink, but Dad insisted that he drink this tea, it was important. Ryan complied, sipping it slowly. Heat coursed through his body and sweat started draining out of every pore. This also made him tired. But this was a different sort of tired, so he relaxed and let whatever was happening to happen.

His mom noticed the wound draining right away. She showed Dad the bandages with the green liquid soaking through. Dad assured them that everything was okay.

Years later, Ryan only remembers moments: Dad handing him the tea. A patched something being placed on his chest. The blazing heat that seared through his body. Lifting his head and swearing in front of his mom, mumbling an apology. Dad speaking his Native tongue, not having any idea what he was saying, and his parents looking over him, watching. Finally, he remembers answering Dad's question about whether he was okay or not.

The Holmans thanked Dad kindly as he left that day. Russell was so overwhelmed with gratitude that he wanted to cry. Even years later, he chokes up remembering that night. Dad reminded them to make sure Ryan finished the entire batch of tea and encouraged them to make sure he continued to rest, even when he started feeling better. Dad knew Ryan, and that as a spirited eighteen-year-old, he would want to hop out of bed as soon as he could.

That night, Ryan's wound drained two quarts of liquid and infection. It had finally begun to heal.

Dad called and checked on Ryan daily, bringing over another batch of tea and continually encouraging him to rest and get well. Within two weeks, Ryan was ready to get out of bed. After seeing him bedridden for nearly three months, the Holman's were overjoyed. There was no doubt in their mind that Gene Goodsky and the Holy Spirit had healed their son.

Dianna Good Sky

They took him to the doctors in Duluth because, as Russ said later, they wanted to get him fully checked out by the medical doctors, both for confirmation of the wound healing, and to share what had happened to him. All the doctors could tell him was to continue to do whatever the healer had told him to do. Ryan's progress was remarkable. The doctors were surprised, relieved, and grateful to see Ryan recover. Russell shared with me years later: "I am a Christian and I know your Dad is not. But there is no doubt in my mind that the Holy Spirit was in your Dad that night he healed my son. The Holy Spirit worked through him. I saw it. I felt it. I know it."

As far as Dad is concerned, he left the Holman residence that night confident that Ryan Holman would live, and grateful for the teachings of his ancestors.

2

THE ANCESTORS

Our family is Ojibwe, although the official treaties and documents call us Chippewa. This is a variation that developed over the years thanks to different accents and dialects (say Ojibwe five times fast and you'll get the picture). But we call ourselves *Anishinabeg*—the original people.

We are part of the Bois Forte Band of Chippewa, one of seven Chippewa Reservations scattered across northern Minnesota. While there are Chippewa all across the northern United States and Canada, most of the Bois Forte Band members live in Nett Lake, Minnesota—what we call the Village. Besides supplying the world's finest wild rice, things are a little easier in Nett Lake than other areas of the Rez. There is access to stores and gas, a clinic, other people. It's where we lived for distinct portions of my childhood. It's where I return to when I visit home.

I remember the very first time I heard the story of how our ancestors came to Nett Lake. It was 1991 and I was stationed in Hawaii. In a different time, I would have learned about our history while sitting around a fire, listening to the elders share the story of our people. *"May Wii Zhaa,"* they would have begun. Once upon a time. Instead, I heard the story as an adult, far away from home.

Dad came to visit that year, and I took a break from my Navy duties to take the family to a luau, one of our favorite touristy events. When you live in Hawaii and you get visitors, going to the luau is a normal occurrence. Plus, I had (and still have) a particular love for the Kailua pork, so my motives may have been two-fold. But I digress.

After the obligatory pictures outside with the Hawaiians in traditional attire, we made our way into the feast. We were stopped at the door by more Hawaiians handing out necklaces made from small shells. We call them *miigis*, but the Hawaiians call them *cowrie*. As they tried to put a necklace around my neck, my dad practically jerked it away from them.

"No, thank you," he said, and I looked at him in surprise. "You can't wear these. Only certain people can wear these." Of course, I asked him why. He said that the *miigis* shell was how we, the Anishinabeg, found Nett Lake, and the lands of our tribe. The wearing of these special shells was reserved for those who were "high ranking." I couldn't even begin to grasp what that meant, except that because I couldn't wear them, I obviously wasn't high ranking.

Our people did not originate in the Great Lakes region but migrated years ago from the East Coast of North America. We have been told this migration was 10,000-11,000 years after the great flood. A prophet told our ancestors about "food that grows on water." We call it Wild Rice. The *miigis* was a sacred shell that our people used as they followed the migration from the East Coast, searching for this food that grows on water. The prophet also told them to follow the *miigis* as a sign. As they crossed the lands and the great bodies of water, we call the Great Lakes, the shells appeared to them along the way, and they followed their trail west.

Warrior Spirit Rising

Our people continued on their journey to eventually settle in the area in and around Nett Lake. It is said that when the leader of the group went ahead to scout the area, he could see someone standing on a small island in the middle of the lake. This person was wearing what looked like clothing made from netting, draped across their body. The scout paddled to the island, only to discover that there was nobody there. Instead, he found petroglyphs carved into the rocks.

The people named the island Spirit Island, in honor of the spirit they saw standing there. They chose to name the lake and region Nett Lake because of the net-like clothing that the spirit wore.

The petroglyph rocks have been researched and studied for years, and it was determined that people inhabited Spirit Island thousands of years ago. Not only that, but the wild rice that covers Nett Lake—the largest producer of wild rice in the United States—has been harvested for over 2000 years.

The history of our people is long, and many details have been lost along with the storytelling that once served as the record-keeping of the tribe. But the shell? The *miigis* shell remains sacred to this day, only used by the *Midewiwin*.

Anishinabeg aren't instinctively the type of people to settle in just one place. That part of our history I can relate to. We moved continuously when I was growing up. Partly because my dad was in the Navy, and partly because the government kept promising opportunities beyond the Rez. Those never worked out.

Before Reservations, Anishinabeg roamed the region in small bands made up of several families. Each band would move to a different camp according to the season: fishing the lakes in the summer, harvesting wild rice in the fall, hunting in the winter, and tapping maples each spring. They traveled between the U.S. and Canada long before there was a border. A border many Natives do not recognize, as such, except when forced to follow the laws and rules.

Dianna Good Sky

Every few months, the people would come together at Pow Wows to give thanks for the bounty of that particular season. Nett Lake was one of those gathering places and remains so to this day.

These gatherings not only served as a reason to give thanks to the Creator for the gifts bestowed, but they were gatherings meant to celebrate life. In spring, the Pow Wow is called *Sa gi bah gah*, Moon of the Bursting Buds. It was a time to ask for new birth, new plants, and an abundance of wild rice. Our ancestors made offerings to the spirits as a sign of gratitude.

The fall Pow Wow, *Miigwetch We Siin Ne Wiin*, was eventually shortened to *Miigwetch Manonmin*, thankful for wild rice because it was also the feast to celebrate all the food that was gifted: the fish, the wild rice, the berries. *ObStah Bii Booon Nii Mii Din*, meaning Half Winter Dance, is celebrated in midwinter, a season to come together.

These gatherings also served as a time to reconnect with family. Sort of like glue in the community to keep the traditions alive. A way to pass cultural practices on to children and grandchildren.

As times changed and people were forced to settle on Reservations, our people stayed near the food that grows on water. New laws banned religious ceremonies and forced land ownership. These changes felt strange and illogical to a people accustomed to sharing the land with everything living. How can a person own parts of Mother Earth? What is wrong with God? You worship one, too.

Over a period of two hundred years, the government passed a million little laws that slowly smothered traditions, religion, and the simplest aspects of life.

Performing religious ceremonies or traditional dances would result in imprisonment. Rations were limited or withheld if men refused to cut their hair. There is also documentation that says if an Indian showed up for their rations and could prove that he had white blood, he would get more meat rations. The theme of the law was always the same—it was good to be white.

Warrior Spirit Rising

Eventually, the enforcement of all things Indian was handed over to the Bureau of Indian Affairs. Their solution was simple: what they could not annihilate, they would assimilate. This came in the form of boarding schools.

The common belief of the day was that Indians were savages. Schools were designed to help save them from themselves. In order to truly assimilate the Indians, the children would need to be removed from their family, language, and traditions. Far removed.

By 1891, attendance at boarding school was mandatory. Bureau agents would come to Reservations and drag the children from their families. Rations were withheld or parents were imprisoned if they refused. Some children left and didn't come home for years. Some never returned.

The boarding schools were harsh and unforgiving. Children were forced to cut their hair, wear western clothing, and only speak English. Punishments were doled out in excess, especially for those caught speaking their native tongue. The abuse was rampant—physical, sexual, and emotional, which was the one that had the longest standing impact on their children and grandchildren. Boarding schools are where traditions went to die.

My grandparents attended boarding school, all but my paternal grandmother, Helen. Her family, the Burnsides, were very traditional and she made sure her children knew the culture and language.

The Goodskys were boarding school attendees and while they learned English, they remained a unique blend of partly assimilated Indians who managed to get back home and continue their traditions.

Many, if not most, of the other boarding school Indians, once home, adopted the English language and that of the white culture, forgoing the Indian ways and traditions. Many even forbade their children to learn the Ojibwe language and culture.

Dianna Good Sky

This was the case with my maternal grandmother, Jennie. She was only three years old when she went away to school, and seven when she returned home. But until the day she passed on, she thought that the beatings she took at school for speaking her Native tongue were justified.

She and my grandpa only spoke Ojibwe when they didn't want the kids to hear what they were saying. They refused to allow their children to learn the language and insisted on speaking English at home.

When she was in her sixties, I asked her if she thought the boarding schools were good for the Indians. She paused, bowed her head, and played with the matchstick on her table in the kitchen. Grandma Jennie, Gram, always had a book of matches sitting on the table. Always. Around and around she twirled this matchstick before lifting her head, finally, and told me, "yes." If she hadn't gone to that school, she wouldn't know how to speak English, and she knew her kids wouldn't survive this new world without it.

It was an interesting paradox. She was right in the sense that the Indians did need to learn the new ways and the English language. Yet, in giving up the traditions of our culture, we were giving up a huge part of our identity. I'm not sure she thought of it that way, or felt that she had any choice.

By the time my parents were school-aged, the forced attendance no longer existed for the Bois Forte Reservation, and they were able to avoid the boarding schools. There was a distinct difference between my parents, though. While my mom and her eight brothers and sisters were not allowed to learn the language, the Goodsky family not only spoke the language, but they also taught the children the ways of the Ojibwe. Dad, his siblings, and their cousins all spoke their Native tongue at home and English at the public school they attended. Since the boarding schools were no longer coming to "catch" them, they also practiced the Ojibwe traditions at home, without as much fear of the repercussions.

My siblings and I also avoided the boarding schools, even though it wasn't until 1978—when I was sixteen—that the government decided it was no longer legal to require boarding school attendance.

By that point, however, the damage was done.

I didn't know about the *miigis*—or much of our history, really—until that day in Hawaii. It was during those years away from home that I began to understand how much of the culture I lacked.

As a child, I had little sense of cultural identity save our family values and the seasonal ricing, hunting, and the occasional Pow Wow I managed to attend. Although I didn't understand it at the time, our culture was nearly gone. Very few people still spoke our traditional language. Pow Wows and religious ceremonies were illegal and, therefore, held in private or rarely practiced for a very long time in our community.

At times, Dad tried to teach us some of our heritage. But those moments always coincided with his drinking, and who wants to learn from a drunk? Not me.

Even though so much was taken away, it was there, in the North Woods of Minnesota that a bit of Anishinabe culture survived. Despite the laws and the rules, boarding schools, and the outlawed religion, the heritage of our ancestors managed to get passed on to another generation. A heritage that would eventually bring my dad back from the brink of death and save Ryan Holman's life.

Dianna Good Sky

3
SUGAR BUSH
1942

Dad was born in 1942 in Nett Lake, Minnesota, delivered by his maternal grandmother. His parents named him Eugene Goodsky, but his Indian name was *Day De Gii Guu Neb*—Quick Flying Hawk. Before long, he would be called *Way Jape*, which simply means "quick."

As children, we rarely, if ever, imagine or realize that our parents were children once, too. As I got older, especially, as I opened up to learning from my parents, I started to see them differently. It's hard to fathom my dad as a child, but I have no doubt that he was a cute, dark little Indian running around and playing amongst the trees, hunting, picking berries, fishing. Oh, the fishing!

When Dad was born, the Goodsky family lived in an area called Sugar Bush, some seventeen miles from the Bois Forte Reservation and the village of Nett Lake. They lived, a family of eight people, in a one-room house. It was small with no running water. The little, rickety, wooden shack didn't offer much by way of comfort.

There was a table with a kerosene lamp sitting there, just waiting to be lit, a wood stove that was used for both heating and cooking, some chairs and four beds: one for his parents, one for the boys, one for the girls, and one for blind Uncle Eddie.

When the siblings were old enough, they decided to spruce up the home with whatever bits they could find. They made a paste out of flour and water and glued a homemade wallpaper of newsprint onto the dark, milled boards that were the walls.

Despite its modest size and appearance, the little house sat encompassed by beauty. It faced Pelican Lake, overlooking the clear waters packed with northern pike and crappies. The rest of the almost ninety-acre peninsula was covered in boreal forest, a little stretch of wilderness less than forty miles from Canada. The nearest city was the small town of Orr.

I like to imagine what it must have been like to grow up there, surrounded by trees and water, sheltered from the rest of the world. I wonder if the sound of the wind hitting the bulrushes ever gets old. Do you learn to tune out the gentle splash of blue-winged teal taking off from the lake's surface?

I remember not understanding when my dad and aunts and uncles would say that Sugar Bush was Goodsky land. I had no idea what it meant when they talked about the allotment, and that the government gave it to them because they lived there. Wasn't that nice of them to do that?

Sugar Bush is covered in pines, birch trees, and sugar maples—the trees that give the region its name. Long before the drawing of the lines that encapsulated the area for the Goodskys and their US Government allotment, the land was a sugar camp for our ancestors. They came there every spring to collect the sugary treat that the maple trees offered.

When I asked Dad how our family came to live there, and not just collect maple sugar, he told me that there had been a fire in Nett Lake. At that time, someone had a dream of a white horse. The white horse told them that they must go to Sugar Bush or nearby Indian Point, as the fire would not reach them there. Years later, Dad's cousin's wife frequently saw this white horse when she lived in Sugar Bush. She said it was majestic and magical. She was the only one we knew to have seen this horse's spirit.

It was here, in this magical place, in the early 1930s, that my grandmother saw her first white man.

At that time, Northern Minnesota was already a haven for hunters and fishermen. They came seasonally to take advantage of the land's abundance and my great-grandfather served as their guide. It was one of the few ways that Indians could actually work to earn currency in the new world that was developing all around them.

It was a fine day for hunting, and the family went about their chores while their father took his customers to the best spots to find bluebills and mallards.

She was twelve at the time—my grandmother. Using a makeshift broom, she stood in front of the house, clearing brush when she saw a canoe approach the landing. It was her father, she realized, coming to fetch the lunch he had left behind that morning. As the canoe drew nearer, she could make out the appearance of other men with her father, men in strange clothes with pale skin. She felt a sudden surge of fear and shock, and dropping her broom, she ran screaming into the house. It was an appropriate act and one we find a bit of twisted humor in. She should have run. The white men were coming.

Even the beauty and seclusion of Sugar Bush couldn't hide the Goodskys from the new world growing all around them. Their options for living off the land became increasingly restricted, and they were forced to adopt the currency of the new world: Money.

Most of the census records show that Indians in my great-grandfather's time were wards of the state. The government told them that in exchange for their land, they would provide food, shelter, and doctors (all necessities once the cultural practices were forbidden). This means they were reliant on the government for food, clothing, everything that they could no longer provide for themselves. But the supplies that were promised rarely ever materialized. Once they realized that the U.S. Government's treaty really wasn't working in their favor, they knew that they had to do more to make their lives better for their children.

They turned to logging and guiding as the trade system lost influence. But there were also parts of nature that they realized were a commodity for the white people and they began to sell the very things they once used for sustenance. I like to think it was seasonal, because, well, it's what they knew. They knew the seasons offered certain things and fitting their world into the white man's world, in order to gain the new currency, makes sense.

When my dad was a boy, one commodity was blueberries.

After the sugar maple sap dries up in late spring, the area becomes a haven of berries, the perfect commerce for small, industrious hands. Dad and his siblings would spend three or four weeks of blueberry season picking for Mackie's Resort up in Crane Lake, on the Canadian border.

They were still young—it was the late 1940s. As a family, they'd make the trip from Sugar Bush to Crane Lake, where some of our relatives still lived. The two older girls, Alma and Ellen, preferred to hang out by themselves. Their mom carried the baby, Bonnie, in the *tikanoggen* on her back while picking the berries. Dad liked following his older brother Henry around, much to Henry's displeasure. Dad would insist, however, chasing after his brother to Mackie's with blueberries in tow.

At the resort, each person was given a piece of gum in exchange for their harvest—but it was a trick. They were asked to show their gum after only a few minutes of chewing. If it was still the off-white color of gum, they were paid in full for their berries. If the gum showed blue, however, their payment was reduced. That was the price of nibbling on the merchandise. The adults fared better than the children, of course, but it didn't take Dad long to learn how the game worked.

Dad was always proud to show his wad of clear gum, held out like an offering in his tiny, blueberry-smudged hand. Henry never seemed to fare so well. Which, of course, pissed him off even more.

Dianna Good Sky

I love hearing those two talk about their childhood. Uncle Henry—we call him Uncle, others call him Hank or Whiz—is a prankster and his laugh is contagious. Between the two of them, Uncle and Dad, the stories are simply wonderful to listen to.

In the summer, after blueberry picking season, the family would load up four birchbark canoes and make the journey north and east to Lac La Croix. The small band of Chippewa that live on the Canadian side of the long, border lake shares our traditions as well as our ancestry. The canoe journey from Crane Lake to Lac La Croix takes about four days, two portages, and several miles through the Boundary Waters Canoe Area Wilderness—a preserved waterway in the north eastern part of Minnesota.

Even in those days, traversing the landscape by boat was like traveling back in time. Although Sugar Bush and even the Rez have their own solitude, the sound of human influence fades even further as the canoes travel deep into Minnesota's North Woods. Rivers flow into lakes, where deep blue waters surround countless tree-capped islands and rock formations older than even Anishinabeg history.

Dad and I made the same trip together as well, years later. But in a motorboat, because, well, we have adapted to modern tools. It took four hours rather than four days. Nowadays, we do it as often as we can.

At the start, the Pelican River flows from the lake, exiting into the dense forest that is so common in that part of the state. The tributary reaches northward into the national forest land, where it joins the Vermilion River and eventually flows into Crane Lake on the Canadian border. Once the Boundary Waters are reached, all modern conveniences are forgotten. There are no roads, no cars, no sounds of motors or smell of engine fuel.

The Boundary Waters were carved into the land by centuries of glacial influence. I remember floating past old growth forest on one side and exposed Precambrian bedrock on the other. Somewhere in the hundreds of miles of waterway are rocks covered in pictures painted long, long ago by the expert touch of Anishinabe hands.

I was very impressed with the portages. Where one section of waterway ends, the boats are carried overland to the next access point. Some portages are manned by a single person who lives in a little cabin, with no one and nothing else around. Their work allows us to cross the otherwise impassable land. At these portages, the boats are hoisted overland on a mechanical system of carts and railroad tracks.

There is something simple and wonderful about watching the boat being lifted from the river, water dripping down the sides as it's set on the carrier designed just for watercraft. I liked watching the boat being carried over the crest of the hill, bobbing slightly from side to side, disappearing into the trees.

Now, when we take these trips together, Dad loves to show me the places he and the family used to stop and camp. And he shares stories that were shared with him.

Growing up, the North Woods of Minnesota, and Sugar Bush in particular, wasn't all birds chirping, leaves rustling, and gentle breezes from the lake—for either of us. While I have fond memories of family barbeques and times with cousins, Sugar Bush was also where the family would gather to drink, both in Dad's childhood and my own.

As a young boy, Dad remembers that the adults would always start off the drinking in a good mood. They would be laughing and having a good time. After a few rounds, the laughter would turn into arguments and yelling. As the night wore on, and the alcohol performed its tricks, the kids would get more and more scared. Dad hated being scared of what might happen and he swore he didn't want to be like that when he grew up. The kids learned it was best to stay quiet and they would all crawl into the beds and try to hide. Much like his own children would do years later.

Dianna Good Sky

Drinking was commonplace on the Reservation even though alcohol sales were outlawed in Indian Country. The perception of Indian weakness toward alcohol was already fully developed by the 1600s and Congress made their first attempt at widespread prohibition shortly after the Revolutionary War. The sale and consumption of alcohol became illegal on Reservation lands, much to the annoyance of merchants and tradesmen.

This caused confusion, however, since most Reservations were not even established at that point. How do you limit sales on lands that aren't defined? By 1832 this was no longer an issue. Indian prohibition was federally mandated and included laws banning the sale of alcohol to Native people anywhere, at any time.

There were ways around such laws, though, and the residents of Sugar Bush knew all the best tricks. The most common practice was to make their own home brew, or "Mash." This homemade concoction used raisins to make a pungent, but effective, liquor. After the substance was boiled and drained, the kids were allowed to eat the soaked raisins. Before they were old enough to join in the drinking, the swollen raisins were the only thing about mash they enjoyed.

When the mash ran out, the adults drank with the help of a few local non-Indians—the "Finlanders." These men would buy wine from the Orr liquor store for Dad's parents, aunts, uncles, everyone. The adults made drinking a regular part of their lives.

There was a certain routine Dad came to expect as a child. First, the adults would gather together on the lakeshore, laughing and drinking and having a good time. Then, when it seemed that all the alcohol was finally finished, they would pack up and head inside, producing—from somewhere—another few gallons of liquor. The kids would eventually find their way to the bed and the relative safety of the covers before the laughter died and morphed into drunken anger.

Uncle Whiz told me how the kids were frequently left with blind Uncle Eddie while their parents were drinking elsewhere. He remembers one time, in particular, when the adults left for several days and the kids were hungry. It was too late to go fishing to make something to eat for themselves. They knew their parents sometimes drank with the old Finlander down the road, so Uncle Whiz grabbed Dad and they made their way through the woods to the Finlander's shack. Uncle already understood the importance and responsibility of looking after the other kids. He was six or seven at the time.

They knocked on the door of the shack and were greeted gruffly by the old Finlander "What do ya want?"

Uncle Whiz told him that they were hungry, so he let them into the dim room, where their parents sat drinking. They made their way over to their mom, who turned and asked the Finlander if he had any food that they could eat. He wasn't pleased, but he got up and quickly made sandwiches for the boys. Uncle had to ask for more sandwiches for the girls and for Uncle Eddie. He shoved the sandwiches at them, and then told them to "go on now."

Uncle Whiz said they were happy to have food until they bit into the sandwiches. The meat tasted like raw pork, so they threw it away and just ate the bread as they walked back to their own house. They clung to the bread that was for the girls and blind Uncle Eddie, wishing the meat hadn't been raw, but glad to have something in their bellies.

Their parents came home late that night, sometime after the kids had gone to sleep. Uncle Whiz remembers that day clearly. Dad, who was barely four, does not. I find it hard to imagine the desperation, walking through the dark woods looking for my parents because I was hungry. At least the hunger I felt, years later, was at home, sitting at an empty dining room table.

Dianna Good Sky

4
GRANDFATHER'S CHARCOAL
1950

As his parents' drinking increased, Dad remembers seeking a bit of sanctuary at his Grandpa Burnside's house in Nett Lake. He would take the Nett Lake bus home from Orr school on Fridays and spend the weekend at his grandpa's. He loved spending time there. His grandpa was a happy drunk. Dad preferred that over the late night arguing that often occurred at home. He mostly liked knowing that there would always be food on the table at his grandpa's house.

They had a very special bond, Dad and Grandpa Burnside. While Dad learned Ojibwe and some of the Chippewa traditions at home, many of the traditional teachings came from his mom's family and especially his grandfather. Grandpa Burnside was a medicine man.

The teachings he shared with Dad were from a long time ago. Dad was an eager student, even when he didn't fully understand the lesson being taught.

He loved learning about everything living, and especially enjoyed understanding the Native plants and their different uses.

He took every opportunity to explore new plants and listen to the birds hidden in the trees above him.

During one particular weekend, Dad had one of his more puzzling cultural lessons with his grandfather. The moment somehow marked him, however, and would impact his life years later.

He woke up to the smell of breakfast cooking; bacon, eggs, fried potatoes, and frybread. When his Grandpa finished cooking, he came up by Dad's bedside and spoke in Ojibwe, saying, "Grandchild, wake up. I have something special that I'm going to show you this morning."

Dad got up and went to the outhouse—even the houses in the Village didn't have running water in those days. He came back, washed up in the basin, and sat down for breakfast. His grandfather brought his plate, piled high with eggs, bacon, fried potatoes and frybread, and a glass of tea.

He put the plate in front of Dad, along with a piece of charcoal that was three-quarters of an inch in diameter, about the size of a thumb. He said, "Take your time. Think about this real clear. Take one. Take the dish or take the charcoal." He looked at Dad. "Don't rush. Think about it."

Dad looked at the plate, and all he could think about was how hungry he felt. His stomach was growling. Then he looked at the charcoal, and the glass of water next to it. He sat in silent contemplation and curiosity. *What is this charcoal?*

Slowly, he reached over and picked up the charcoal.

The minute he picked it up, his grandfather took the plate of food and the tea. He left Dad with the charcoal and water, and he said, "Eat this. You won't be hungry. You won't go hungry today."

Dad cautiously picked away at the charcoal. When he finished, his grandpa said, "Now get dressed and go find your friend. You won't go hungry today."

Dad sighed. *Geez.* He thought he was being slick by picking up the charcoal first. Maybe his grandpa would still give him the plate of food. He didn't know what the charcoal was about, at all. But he felt like he should pick it up. So, he did.

After breakfast, he went over to his friend's house and they played together in the back woods. Around noon, his friend's mother hollered for them to come eat lunch. When the boys got inside, she had already set two places, a bowl of wild rice and duck. *Well, that looks good*, thought Dad.

Instead, he shuffled his feet and quietly said, "I'm not hungry."

When you refuse to eat, in our culture, it's an insult to the person that has prepared the food. Dad was embarrassed, so he quickly tried to explain about the charcoal.

She understood right away and cleared Dad's plate away. He sat there puzzled. *What is it that everyone else seems to understand about this charcoal?*

Toward evening, Dad went back home to his grandfather's house. After spending the day confused—and wishing he could eat but likely out of habit more than anything else—he finally asked him, "Grandpa, what does that charcoal mean?"

"In time, you will know. Your answer will come to you. I can't tell you."

Something changed in him. Dad always liked nature, but he became far more interested in living beings, especially birds, animals, and plants. When he would visit the library, he always checked out books that were related to animals, trees, or birds. He wanted to know the names of everything and learn everything he could about the different species. He even began studying their Anishinabe names.

In school, he studied biology, furthering his interest in living things and native plants and animals.

When Dad was ten years old, his grandfather passed on. Dad was not able to attend the funeral because he had not yet become a man. These days, they allow children to attend funerals, using charcoal to protect them from being taken early.

He regretted not seeing his grandfather to say goodbye. He didn't believe his grandpa was gone, and he was overwhelmed by loneliness.

Years later, he shared the story of his grandfather and the charcoal with another medicine man. He still didn't know what it meant or why that moment sparked his interest in nature. The medicine man looked at him and said, "You will know when the time comes." Then he looked up above him, pointing upwards with his bottom lip, as is customary. "He will give you the answer. Your answer will come to you."

Dianna Good Sky

5

CHANGES
1953

The year Dad turned eleven, prohibition in Indian Country was finally repealed. It was 1953, a full twenty years after federal prohibition ended for the rest of the United States—and over 120 years after prohibition for Indians began. At least we fared better than our family to the north. Canada's prohibition didn't end for their First Nation tribes until 1985.

They say the law was changed because of patriotism, or something like that. After the war, it was argued that if Indians can serve the country—over 44,000 fought in World War II—they should be able to legally drink.

For centuries, the narrative around Indians and alcohol has been dominated by stereotypes. Genetic predisposition, inability to cope with cultural change, inherent addictive behavior—all ideas that tell a similar story as the laws and cultural restrictions: to be Indian is a weakness. To be white is good. The truth is, restrictions on alcohol only add to the feeling of need or desperation, which then increases the use (or in this case, abuse).

Even though the sale of alcohol to Indians became legal, the narrative—and many other restrictions—remained. Since Indians exhibited a supposed weakness toward alcohol, while they could legally buy and drink it, they certainly could not be trusted to produce it. That law, the one that kept Indians from distilling liquor on Reservation lands, was only repealed in December 2018.

When the prohibition law finally changed in 1953, however, the social identity around drinking on the Bois Forte Rez was already established. At that point, things got really crazy both in Nett Lake and in Sugar Bush. No longer having his safe haven at his grandpa's house in Nett Lake, Dad would still occasionally ride the bus to the Village on the weekends to play with his friends. It wasn't the same for him after his grandpa passed, not at all. At least he could escape what was happening in the tiny cabin at Sugar Bush for a bit, even if that respite didn't last very long.

Dad's life in Sugar Bush wasn't only marked by drinking, however. This somewhat secluded life in Sugar Bush was home to one of the greatest gifts my dad and his siblings could ever hope for: the passing on of traditions. The Ojibwe culture and ways of living that were slowly dying also managed to get passed down to Dad and his siblings. This is because Dad's mom, Helen, who was Grandpa Burnside's daughter, helped keep many of the cultural traditions alive in our family, influenced by her father's role as a medicine man.

Helen's Indian name was *Bay Ba Gah Mah Tay Bi Nay Zeek*— Red Sunrise. Everyone called her Gahmaht. It's customary to use shortened names, just like we do in English; shortening Jacob to Jake, Dianna to Di. You get the idea. My grandma Gahmaht died while I was stationed in Hawaii. She is buried in a red dress, in honor of her name.

Her husband, Dad's father, was named *Be Da Tay Gah Bouw*— Just before the Sunrise. A fitting name for the man married to Red Sunrise. They called him Gah Bouw, but some friends used to call him Cowboy, in jest. His English name was Henry. I never met my grandfather; he died before I was born.

Dianna Good Sky

Dad remembers that Gah Bouw used to tell him, "take care of yourself." The words never really had meaning for him until years later. But Dad likes to say that children store the things their parents say. They store it in the back of their minds and bring it out when they are ready and able to truly understand the meaning.

Helen and Henry—Gahmaht and Gah Bouw—created a unique blend of the old Indian ways and the ways of the new white world in their home. Dad and his siblings spoke Ojibwe at home and English at school. But they also understood the value of building relationships with everyone, regardless of race, religion, or culture.

This was especially valuable in their relationship with the Richardsons, the white neighbors across the bay from Sugar Bush. The Richardsons began building a resort off Sugar Bush Trail when Dad and his siblings were still young—before prohibition ended. Before Grandpa Burnside passed on. They hired Dad and Uncle Whiz, along with cousin Harold—who everyone called Dayshun—to help. Dad is very proud of the fact that he learned how to drive a truck, at about the age of nine, while working for the Richardsons.

The resort was to become a destination for families and fishermen looking to enjoy a quiet, secluded vacation on the lake. The boys worked hard at the resort, hauling huge stones to line the driveway, clearing debris, and even building. They enjoyed the chance to work, learn, and earn some money. Dad said the money they made was contributed to the household. They would get a few treats from their work money, but that didn't matter to them. They were proud to help support the family.

Working for the Richardson's had its perks. One of which was learning about carpentry. Dad loved learning how to use a tube of water as a leveler while building the cabins. As a boy, he was very impressed with how Mr. Richardson did that trick. His passion for carpentry and building stuck with him, eventually influencing his decision to become a Seabee in the US Navy. Apart from learning new skills and helping the family, frankly, Dad and Uncle also loved how well they were treated there. They were never hungry while at the Richardson's.

They worked there every summer. As long as the Richardson family needed help, they were there to provide it.

Richardson's Shangri-La Resort sits directly across the water from Sugar Bush. When I visit, I enjoy sitting on Dad's dock and watching the people come and go across the bay. It is now run by the third generation of Richardsons; the relationship between our families has lasted to this day.

I met a woman, many years later, who, after finding out I was from the North Woods of Minnesota, told me a story about her childhood. When she was about five or six, her family went on a vacation up in the deep woods of Minnesota. The area was barely inhabited, and the cabins were very rustic, but she never forgot that trip for two reasons: the natural beauty was unlike anywhere she had ever been, and there were two young Indians boys working their tail off for the resort. She remembered thinking how cute they were and wondering how it was that her family was vacationing while these young boys were working so hard. It impressed her so much that she distinctly remembered those boys forty-five years later. She couldn't confirm the resort—she was too young to remember those details—but I would like to think that it was the Richardson's resort. That was the moment I started to realize that my drunk, stern dad, was once a cute little boy.

Relationship building with the white folks was nothing new to Dad. The only Indians who attended Orr school at the elementary grades were those who lived in Sugar Bush and nearby Indian Point. From the moment they entered first grade, the Sugar Bush Indians were exposed to a culture vastly different from their own.

Racism doesn't come naturally to humans, though, so getting along with the other kids at school was something that Dad and the other kids just...did. Racism, however, can be taught.

Dianna Good Sky

Dad's worst experience with racism came from the Nett Lake students. Nett Lake Indians were bussed into Orr school starting in the seventh grade. The transition was challenging for both the Nett Lake students and the Indians who had already attended Orr school for years.

When Dad reached seventh grade, there were several Nett Lake students who liked to taunt him. They called him "apple." You know, red on the outside but white in the middle. They mocked him because he got along so easily with the white kids. They also teased him about getting good grades. Dad felt compelled to lower his grades to reduce the teasing. That's a normal reaction, right? Lowering personal standards to fit in? He never wanted to get good grades again.

His parents told him to try to ignore the bullies, but he decided there was only one way to make them stop. So, one day, he hauled his right arm back and punched B.D.—his main opposition—straight in the nose. Ta Da! No more bullying from the Indians. It was the only time and place he experienced bullying. The racism, however, would follow him far beyond Orr School.

In the summertime, he didn't have to worry about his troubles at school. The Richardson family really appreciated the Goodsky family, and all their help with the growing resort. The money they earned came in very handy as Dad and his siblings got older. It helped fill the financial gap the family suffered due to increased cost of living in an isolated area, and the family's growing reliance on store-bought goods as the old ways of hunting and gathering started slipping away.

They could no longer rely on having time to hunt and gather anymore. Gah Bouw had to get a regular job and the kids were busy attending school in Orr. Fewer and fewer people were hunting and sharing the bounty, as was custom. And money was slipping away along with the increased alcohol consumption, once the alcohol laws changed.

By the time he was a young teenager, Dad's family had been legally purchasing alcohol for nearly four years, but their routine was still very much the same: drinking, laughing, arguments, passing out. After what he witnessed through his childhood years, even before the laws changed, Dad made a promise to himself that he would never drink in excess. One night, things changed.

Everyone in the house was drinking that night, including his older siblings and their friends. Most were in their laughing, jovial stage of the process when they cajoled Dad into joining them. He drank about three beers with them before needing to use the bathroom. On his way across the room, he realized he couldn't walk straight, and everyone started laughing at him as he stumbled toward the outhouse. After two more beers, he started to feel really bad, so he stumbled outside and fell in the field, heaving. He could hear everyone inside laughing.

He felt terrible. Eventually he got up and made his way to the lakefront where he fell to the ground and decided that he may as well stay there. Dad fell asleep with the sound of laughter ringing in his ears. When he woke up, he felt even worse. He promised himself, again, that he would never drink like that, like the others. He was fifteen. Cultural influence—and life circumstances—though, are powerful.

In August of 1958, Gahmaht and Gah Bouw were out drinking. The kids stayed home with blind Uncle Eddie.

Dad and the others woke up to the sound of someone banging on the front door. Startled, they stumbled to the door in a jumble of groggy, teenage confusion.

Ira Isham, the Nett Lake Sheriff, stood in the darkness of the front step. He was accompanied by another uniformed police officer.

"I have some bad news for you kids," he said quietly. He paused, cautious. "Your dad got run over by a train."

Dianna Good Sky

His words hung there, like in a void, and then disappeared into the night.

Everything and everyone stood silent for a single heartbeat. It felt like a lifetime. Then the girls started screaming.

Their wails echoed across Pelican Lake. Even the trees couldn't escape the sound of their pain.

The boys stood silent. Stoic. They were raised to believe that men don't cry.

The first time Dad told me this story, he mentioned that, of course, that was wrong. Boys should be able to cry. It just wasn't like that for them.

Despite that, Uncle Whiz took off into the woods and privately cried his eyes out. He kept crying and crying—he couldn't stop. He could hear the others calling for him, but he couldn't let them see him like that, so he didn't answer their calls. He cried in the woods for a long time. Finally, toward daylight, Uncle Gordy found him and brought him back to the house.

Sheriff Ira stayed until the kids got settled and Gahmaht and the aunts and uncles started showing up at the house. They stayed up all night—the girls couldn't seem to calm down until cousin Myrna, from just down the street, came over to distract them. Myrna was very funny, a little crazy and always fun to be around. She was able to help the girls process some of their grief that night.

The boys, on the other hand, along with cousin Dayshun, decided to bike into Orr. They didn't believe their dad was gone. Shock will do that to a person.

They biked the five miles into Orr, only stopping once they reached the train tracks. Sheriff Ira told them that the incident happened right across the street from the little motel. The scene was horrific.

They stared in disbelief at chunks of meat and fat scattered everywhere. And the blood. So much blood.

I can't even imagine the horror.

Despite seeing the evidence for themselves, it still took them a long time to get over Gah Bouw's passing. Of course. For the longest time, Dad and his siblings would expect him to walk home from work, carrying the groceries and firewood for the kitchen stove. He never came, Dad said. He just never came.

Ira suspected foul play. He said he had never seen Gah Bouw passed out (laid out, we usually say) anywhere before. Why would he start now?

That night, Gahmaht and Gah Bouw had been drinking in Orr with Auntie Martha and Uncle Gordy. Gordy used to work at Stagburgs lumber yard, just like Gah Bouw, and they lived in a cabin near the job site in Orr. There were other people there, as well, and my grandpa had left with a couple of other men late in the evening.

Ira believed that at some point, those men got into a fight. Grandpa got beaten up, he suspected, and then left there on the railroad tracks. Ira tried to investigate, but there were no leads. There was never any resolution to Gah Bouw's death.

It landed on Uncle Whiz to take care of the family. As the oldest boy—he was seventeen years old—he had to drop out of school and work full time to try to support the family. So, he replaced my grandpa working at Stagburgs. Yet, his salary wasn't enough, so Dad also started working part time at Stagburgs lumber yard after school. Things changed dramatically for the family.

When I asked my dad and Uncle what they remembered most about their dad, they both said, "Trust. He taught us the value of trust." I asked them at two different times, different locations, and they were alone with me when they answered my question. I was very impressed that this was their father's legacy.

When I asked them to explain how he taught them trust, their answers were also basically the same. Gah Bouw used to give them .22-gauge rifles, with five bullets each, and send them off to kill dinner. Both of their parents would also simply trust them to take out the canoe, and all they would ever tell them was to "take care

Dianna Good Sky

of things." It's a lesson both Gahmaht and Gah Bouw passed on to their children.

Dad and Whiz also both remember that their dad would wait up for them when the boys were at sporting events. He would always be sitting there at the little table with the kerosene lamp, smoking a cigarette, waiting for the boys to get home from their five-mile walk from school. What a beautiful memory that must be. If he had had a car, I am certain Dad's parents would have attended these events. They were very supportive and proud of their boys' athletic abilities.

At the time of his father's passing, Dad was about to enter the tenth grade at Orr school. He was an excellent athlete, he especially loved playing basketball. He played for the school team and worked hard at it, too. His love for the game showed in his skill. He admired his coaches very much and wanted to learn all that he could from them. And so, he did.

He put his enthusiasm and hard work into everything he did, including the traditional ricing at the end of each summer. Because of the cultural importance of ricing to the local families, the schools would excuse the Bois Forte students from classes for the entire month of September.

Back then, ricing season in Nett Lake was much like I experience it today. Most people would rice for family food, but after enough was gathered to feed the family, the remaining rice was sold for profit. The excess income meant a sudden increase in purchasing across the Village. Parents buy school clothes for the kids, and teenagers spend their money on everything necessary and useless, as if tomorrow might never arrive.

For decades, the order of ricing season financial priority has remained the same: family food, new-old car, school clothes, liquor. Oh, and parties all around the Village. Not to mention the "ricing babies"; kids born nine months from the ricing season. There are always ricing babies.

Warrior Spirit Rising

Dad was sixteen that ricing season, after his dad passed on. He worked hard to get enough rice to buy his own new-old car. A car offered some freedom. He took care of that, which meant the next priority for ricing money was clothing and then partying. Dad had avoided drinking with the others after his humiliation the year before, but this year was different. Things had changed so much; he rather enjoyed the escape the partying with his peers offered him.

He and Whiz had discovered a bar in the deep woods that would serve them beer even though they were still underage. So, every day after ricing they drove out to the bar. When it closed at one a.m. Dad and Uncle Whiz took a bunch of cases of beer and went back to the Rez. Most days they did not get a lot of sleep and by the next morning, they would head back out onto the lake, still hammered. They did that all month long.

They say it takes twenty-one days to form a habit. The truth is, it can take anywhere from two days to eight months, depending on the habit. By the end of that ricing season in September, Dad's promise to himself was a distant memory. He joined the adults and the cousins in the family routine: drink, drink some more, and then drink until the world fades into oblivion.

It was a simple habit to form. From that time on, drinking was a normal part of his life. But Dad thought he had a grip on it since he was still able to go to school, play sports, and study. He didn't want the drinking to interfere with that.

When his mom decided to get a house in the Village, however, things changed again. Gahmaht moved to Nett Lake with thirteen-year-old Bonnie, the youngest, and her only girl who was not yet married. Uncle Whiz moved out to his own place, and Dad chose to go with him.

It wasn't long before Dad felt that high school was not worth his time. His work at Stagburgs offered him steady pay, which gave him freedom, and the ability to help his mom, who was having trouble making ends meet.

Dianna Good Sky

He dropped out of school before he had finished the tenth grade. Things—school, sports, life— didn't seem to matter as much as they used to, when his dad was alive.

Sugar Bush, named for the abundance of maple trees, the place the Goodsky's had called home for so many years, became a distant memory. I suppose life moves on, or at least that's what we tell ourselves.

6
SERVICE TO COUNTRY
1959

Dad remembers his high school Biology teacher once asking him: "Do you think you will ever amount to anything?"

"I hope so." Dad replied.

It didn't take Dad long to realize that he had to escape the Reservation if he wanted to "amount to anything." The Rez is isolated, which means jobs are hard to come by, and the jobs that were available didn't interest him in the least. He had to get away from home.

Like many others before him, the military offered an escape. As a Native American, it was also in his blood to be a warrior. It made perfect sense to defend the United States: Dad is as patriotic as they come.

What he really wanted to do was work in construction. It was something he loved ever since he was a boy working for Richardson's resort. He was also very good at it. The Navy has special construction units called the Seabees, and so Dad chose to join the Navy. He was only seventeen years old.

Because of his age, Gahmaht had to sign the papers saying it was okay for him to join as a minor, and she did so gladly. It had been eight months since his father passed on and she knew he needed to get away. Dad wanted to join the military and she was happy for him.

When he talked to the Navy recruiter, however, Dad learned that there were no Seabee billets available—but he was desperate. Whiz's tiny shack was feeling overly crowded and he was itching to make a life for himself. So instead, he joined with a fireman designation. His actual job title was a Machinist Mate (MM rating).

The Navy was a very different life than what Dad was used to, but he was determined to stick with it. While he missed home and his family, he soon found that the Navy offered certain freedoms— and a steady paycheck. That was a nice benefit. As a single man just starting out, that money freedom meant going to the club and having a good time.

Once he finished training, Dad's first station was aboard the USS *Princeton*. The USS *Princeton* was conducting WESTPAC Operations (Western Pacific) at the time, and it was also a troop carrier and sometimes transferred Marine Corps personnel from Camp Pendleton to Vietnam. At one point, Dad's ship just so happened to carry his brother Whiz's battalion. It wouldn't be the first nor the last time that young men from Nett Lake ran into each other while serving—whether it was Mississippi, California, on ships, or especially in Vietnam.

The USS *Princeton* was just one of several units involved in the Atomic Bomb testing in the Pacific Ocean. They were told they couldn't talk about their involvement to anyone nor could they record it in any way, and they all had to sign documents to that effect.

As a matter of fact, most records of the USS *Princeton* have zero mention of its participation in Operation Dominic and the 1962 tests in the Pacific. I had no idea, myself, as Dad did as he was told and never mentioned it. It wasn't until 2017, as I sorted through some of his records that my mom had kept, that I found his Princeton paperwork and started doing a bit of research. I discovered that Operation Dominic was declassified, and the ban lifted in 1996, and after letting Dad know, he felt free to tell me all about it. They are called "Atomic Vets."

Dad remembers that during the testing, they were told to crouch down with their knees up and their heads tucked between their legs with their arms wrapped around the knees. They were also told they couldn't look at the bomb going off in the ocean, but of course they did. The boom from the explosion was deafening and the mushroom cloud was a sight he will never forget. He said he couldn't believe how big that cloud was.

They had positioned the ship sideways, so even with their eyes supposedly covered, they could all see the shockwave coming through the water. The explosion caused a massive ripple effect in the water and it rocked the ship so hard they feared it would tip the ship, or at least knock them over. As Dad opened his eyes and reached out to grab hold of something, anything to keep him from falling, he recalls that his arm looked almost like it was fluorescent. After the ship and the bomb both settled, the crew couldn't help but talk about what was in that cloud. The corpsman—from the medical unit—said that eventually it would catch up to them.

Of course, it did. It was atomic radiation. They had no idea just how much danger they were in, nor of the subsequent fallout of being so close to the explosions. Today, the Department of Defense estimates that some 550,000 men and women were exposed to radiation while serving the U.S. between 1945 and 1992. Another nearly half a million were exposed just during World War II alone.

When the Atomic Vets were on shore, they were able to go on liberty and they always hit the local bars. There was no drinking age restriction for those in the military. It was during this time that Dad feels he became addicted to alcohol. For him, it was an endless cycle of duty days and liberty in foreign ports, with nothing better to do but drink and escape.

Dianna Good Sky

Fairly soon after the Atomic tests, his enlistment orders were complete and even though he liked some of the benefits the Navy offered, being a Machinist Mate was not really what he wanted to be doing. Plus, during his time at home on leave, he managed to pick up a wife and child. Now, his wife was expecting another baby—it was time to go home.

7
RESERVATION AND RELOCATION
1963

GRowing up, I wasn't always embarrassed by my dad. But I certainly didn't see him as any particular representation of Indian culture. He was just Dad. Yes, a full-blooded Indian, but just Dad. He worked hard and drank hard just like the rest of them. There was even a time, before he became the town drunk, when we were just a normal family. Or, as normal as any other military family.

I spent the first few years of my life on the Rez. When Dad got out of the Navy, he returned to us—me, Mom, and my soon-to-be-born sister—and the Reservation. He started work as a carpenter in Nett Lake Village. He loved the job. The tribe had received funding, from somewhere, to build new houses, meaning there was plenty of work to be had.

We also lived up in the Village, next door to Grandma and Grandpa King and Uncle Whiz and Aunt Lela (my mom's sister Lela, married my dad's brother Hank, Isn't that great?). We spent much of our time with Lela and Whiz's four children. We call them double cousins, but they're more like brothers and sisters, even more so than our other cousins. I loved living there. There was still no running water and we had to use the outhouse, but I didn't know there was anything different. We were, however, moving toward modernization. We had electricity and even a television. It was here that we watched the footage of JFK getting shot. We loved that old house.

Anything resembling stability, however, was always short lived. If there was any constant in our lives, it was rules and change; the benchmark of a military family.

Dad was home for almost a year when word started getting around about a new program that was being offered to the Indians. They were advertising a vocational training program. At first, it looked great. The program would pay you to move to a big city and get training for a trade. That's what Dad says they advertised to him, and, according to Dad, Mom fell for the advertising. The truth is, it turned out to be part of the Indian Relocation Act of 1956. The real goal behind the program, and its forerunner, House Concurrent Resolution 108, was to wean people off the Reservation and entice them to assimilate into life in the city. Much like the legislation of the previous hundred years—including the boarding schools—the overarching objective was the eradication of Indian culture, tribes, and lands. These came to be known as termination policies.

Dad was happy to stay a carpenter in Nett Lake, but Mom thought the trade school program sounded really good, like something they should do; get away from the Reservation and go to a city. After a bit of a struggle, Mom won out and Dad chose to apply for barber school. The school was in San Francisco, California.

Dad drove us to California in a little Ford with a U-Haul pulled behind. The government gave him mileage, which paid for the gas in the car, and they also promised to pay for housing and a monthly stipend to live on until he could get trained and find a job.

I think there must have been a few lucky recipients of this program, because I remember our little house in San Francisco—

an apartment complex—and it was not bad at all. It certainly had running water. We were introduced to indoor plumbing as a result of this program. That was nice.

The San Francisco apartment was in a high-rise building. It had a great view and while the furniture was sparse, it was clean and decent. I am fairly certain it was a very exciting time. First, driving across the country, especially since my sister and I had only ever been as far as Minneapolis. Then, arriving in the big city with all its lights, and the Golden Gate Bridge a majestic red arc over the water. I will never forget seeing all the city lights of San Francisco. When you've only seen the deep woods of Minnesota, city lights are a huge deal. My sister, Lela, and I got into big trouble one night as we tried to look at them closer.

We went out on the forbidden balcony (which was *very* high up) while Mom was busy with something else. But then, we heard her calling for us. We looked at each other with those "Uh-oh" eyes and wanted to hide. But, where could we go? We were on a balcony on a high-rise building, in San Francisco. Mom's voice was getting louder and I could tell she was worried. All we could do was crouch down. She finally opened the balcony door and, well, have you ever heard a worried mom yelling with relief and joy at the same time? Which then turns to anger as she realizes how you blatantly disobeyed her? Yep. It was like that.

From that point on, we had to enjoy the lights from the living room window. But hey...we had an indoor toilet! I can only imagine how amazing that must have been for my mom—to not worry about us falling in the outhouse hole. Or emptying the slop pail. Certainly, it all seemed new to me.

We got settled in and Dad went to barber school. He had to commute in the little Ford because the school was in Oakland. And it didn't take long for him to get tired of commuting after his already long training days. So, my parents decided to move from San Francisco to Oakland.

I don't remember the home in Oakland very well. The stipend wasn't much—in many cities that offered the program, it barely covered the overpriced housing—but my parents made do on what they had, and I don't remember ever going hungry. It must have been a decent program.

The only problem was that Dad's feet went out on him after six weeks in the barber school. He couldn't handle standing for that long; the training and practice times were over eight hours a day. He thinks it had something to do with his time in the military as a Machinist Mate on the USS *Princeton*. He's not exactly sure what happened to his feet, he just knows his feet basically stopped, they were hurting too bad. He couldn't stand up, barely moving, for that long every day.

Dad left the barber school and went to the program manager to find out what other schools were available to him. He didn't want to have to move again. The adjustment to indoor plumbing was great, but we were all having a hard time adjusting to the area. My parents didn't feel comfortable outside of their home. We had no friends nearby, although my mom's brother, Uncle Arnold, and his buddy, Elmer Gonier, did come out to visit for a while. It was nice to see familiar faces.

Before we left Minnesota, my parents had been told that there would be many other people from Nett Lake using the program, but there really weren't that many. Certainly, none that had come to Oakland. Dad said there *were* a lot of Indians there, but they all had their own language and backgrounds. Just because they were Indians didn't mean they would automatically get along. Common misunderstanding of the Indians, I guess. Or blatant lies. Honestly, maybe it was the hope of the government that it would be that way. That people would move away from the Reservations together in droves.

The program emphasized specific cities that were available for relocation, and to this day, most of those cities have a large contingent of Indians. Yet, most of those urban Indian populations are in poverty, even now.

In Oakland, many of the relocated Indians lived in the black ghetto, so the Indian ghetto was two times removed from mainstream society. It became abundantly clear that the government's program was not built to assist or support, but simply to remove the Indian's from Reservation lands and lessen their reliance on the government. Most of the time it didn't work, including in our case.

After the issue with his feet, Dad applied to go to mechanic school. It took a little while for them to get him in, but they soon found him a program. Oakland was a big recipient of a large number of Indians. It certainly was the beginning of the huge Indian population in the Oakland area. This particular program, especially, did succeed in that manner.

While I don't remember a lot from that season in the Bay Area, I do remember the parties. Besides Mom's brother and his friend visiting, we also found out that Mom's cousin, Uncle Edwin Porter, was stationed at NAS Miramar, and he would sometimes come over with his steel guitar. In spite of everything, those were happy times. Even I remember all the joy and laughter during that time.

We were on the West Coast for almost a year, but aside from the happy memories of family visits, things were just not as great in the big city as we were made to believe. Even with the stipend, there wasn't enough to feed a family of four comfortably. And while Dad was progressing in trade school, they realized that the chances of getting a well-paying job afterward were slim. After a while, my parents didn't feel good being there. They realized that it was a mistake.

The relocation program was strategic in its approach, however. While money was freely offered for travel *to* the city of choice, return fare was not. For many, saving enough to get back home was nearly impossible. There are those who, despite the conditions and low wages, simply never left. They couldn't.

My parents were fortunate. When they decided we would return home, they had one stipend check left. It was enough to purchase bus tickets for me, Mom, and my sister.

Dianna Good Sky

It was an odd situation, that bus trip from Oakland to Minneapolis. Mom kept pointing out the window to distract us. "Look how pretty that is," she would say, and, "Oh, look over there. It's beautiful!" I'm sure I got that from her. I still do that with my kids and grandkids.

My mom was a brave woman. I would never have taken the bus cross country with kids, and certainly not as an Indian in the 1960s. Neither Lela nor I understood what it really meant. Why was dad in the car? Why were we leaving the city? It would only be years later that we would begin to realize the implications of that season.

Once all of our belongings were piled into the Ford and the U-Haul trailer, Mom hadn't felt comfortable putting us in the overloaded car. That's why we took the bus and Dad drove. But because we had very little money from the last stipend, after buying the bus tickets and food, Dad barely had enough money to make it home himself.

He got as far as Grand Rapids, Minnesota—about an hour and a half from Nett Lake—when he had to stop. He had about a quarter tank of gas left and he knew he wouldn't make it. Dad pulled into a gas station and asked the attendant, "Would you give me some gas for my spare tire?" The man said, "But what if you get a flat tire?" Dad said, "Well, I'll have to take that chance. I don't have no money."

After filling up, Dad was somewhere between the final stretch of Highway 65 and the road to Nett Lake when he saw a porcupine and he stopped. Porcupine quills are used for regalia and jewelry; they are quite prized. So, when Dad saw this little porcupine alone on the side of the road, he decided to bring it home and give it to his mom.

We were so excited to see him after the long trip across the country, but when he showed us the porcupine, our attention was immediately drawn to the cutest creature we had ever seen. We begged to pick it up, and of course he wouldn't let us.

He was going to take it to his mom the next day, so he put the porcupine in a box and placed it somewhere safe. The next morning, he went to get his gift, but the porcupine had chewed a hole through the box and escaped. He thought it was the funniest thing. When he told his mom about it, she just said, "That's good. You can't keep wild animals like that. They don't belong in a box. It's like a prison and they don't belong there. So, good for the porcupine. I'm glad he got away!"

In many ways my parents were lucky—we all were—to have made it back. In fact, they knew they could always come home. Many of the Indians who participated in the relocation program did not have that luxury. They were trapped in their own boxes, ones uniquely crafted by the U.S. government.

Today, this immobility seems very normal of Native Americans, except it happens in reverse. They can't leave home. If they do leave home, they somehow always make their way back. Part of that is they just don't feel right about being away from home, being in a different community where everything is so foreign. Native Americans have the highest rate of any group, per capita, of serving in the military. They also have the lowest retention rate. They join, but they don't stay. Our box, the Reservation, is what we know, and it's an odd thing to be so far removed from home.

Dianna Good Sky

8
U.S. NAVY SEABEE
1966

Returning home to the Reservation, Dad got his job back working as a carpenter. The Tribe was still building houses in the Village, indoor plumbing was becoming a reality for many, and so, there was plenty of work available for him. He loved carpentry, and he was really happy to be home.

After a few years of being a civilian, a friend told Dad about the Construction Battalion in the Navy. They were called Seabees, the program Dad had originally wanted when he first joined the Navy. He remembered the security of the military and the good times and felt very strongly that he would love doing construction work on active duty.

The only catch was that he would almost likely be immediately sent to Vietnam.

He attended Seabee boot camp in Gulfport Mississippi and earned his Expert Rifleman and Pistol Sharpshooter badges. He also received one week of survival training...yep, he was going to Vietnam.

The survival training included a Compass course and an Escape and Evasion course. During the Escape and Evasion course, the invaders were Marines. They represented the enemy during this part of the training.

At one point during the survival training, Dad noticed a group of crows. He asked his Company Commander (CC) if he could go check out what the crows were after. The CC gave him permission and Dad went to look for whatever the crows were flying toward. He found a dead deer with only a little of the body eaten away by the birds. Dad skinned the deer and cut it up, stripping the meat off the bones with his K-Bar. That night, his company boiled the meat for dinner. They were the only company to have such good food during the survival training, which was a dream come true, because they were all simply starving. Dad knew his brothers in arms were really happy that he was with them.

On the last day, they were captured. They were taken into a mock POW camp where they were tortured. Prior to this, they had to sign a paper saying they would not hit back. So, the training involved real hitting and real torture in anticipation of the war in Vietnam and the possibility of being captured. There were at least five men who didn't make it through this part of the training. Dad never saw them again.

After the POW simulation, the Company Commander marched them in front of the U.S. Flag. He gave the command to "Present arms" and they held their rifles in front of them as a salute. He then reminded them that this—the flag, the country, and all those who lived in America—is what they were fighting to protect.

Dad still gets choked up talking about that day.

It was while Dad was in Gulfport that he saw a familiar face. It wasn't the first time he had encountered people from Nett Lake in other parts of the world, and it wouldn't be the last. But this was a particularly memorable connection. Russ Holman was about three weeks ahead of Dad in boot camp. They had both attended Orr High School, and their families—the Goodskys and the Holmans—were old friends. Dad and Russ managed to chat for a few minutes before parting ways. Russ was already on his way to Vietnam and they would not see each other again until after they both returned home. But it was not the last time their lives would be inextricably connected.

After Dad was trained and ready to go to Vietnam, he was able to take thirty days of leave to go home. It was during this leave that my Mom got pregnant again, this time with my brother (I tease him that he must have been a going away gift). The doctor at the local clinic offered to hold Dad back from the war because he was married with children, but he declined. He was, after all, committed to the Navy and to the country. He was proud to be of service and while he didn't look forward to war, it was what he signed up for.

While home on leave, there were several special ceremonies conducted for him. One was held by Walter Caribou and Jesse Drift, two family friends who had been raised in the traditional ways, like Dad. They gave him an Eagle feather for protection. Then they told him that whenever he gets in trouble, he should offer tobacco and then face the east, south, west, north, up, down, and below and he would be okay.

When Dad was still in boot camp, another member of the tribe had a dream about him. This man, Henry Geyshick, immediately called Gahmaht and told her that he had a dream about her son, Gene.

"I dreamt about your son," he said. "It's going to be tough ahead, where he's going. His spirit has come to me. He had brown buckskin pants, long white hair, and in this vision, your son had his rifle, helmet, and his backpack and there was a wolf on the other side of him. 'I need to go with him,' the wolf said, 'Because he will be going through some rough spots.' The white-haired man walked away and only the wolf and your son were left standing."

Henry then explained to Gahmaht that they had to do a ceremony when Gene came home, so the wolf could go with him.

Henry performed the ceremony. The family gathered— Gahmaht and her new husband, Russell, Henry Geyshick and his wife, and several others—and ate from the ceremonial dish. They each took a little sip of a drink as part of the ceremony and Henry told Dad, "There, he is with you. But you have to feed him meat, he's a meat eater."

Once in Vietnam, Dad did what he was told, and he would give an offering of tobacco for protection. Occasionally, to honor the wolf, he would add some meat to his tobacco ceremonies.

One of the Lieutenants saw him use the tobacco and said: "I see you putting tobacco down before we head out on a mission, what are you doing?" So, Dad told him.

"Would it work for me?" He asked. Dad said if he believed, then it would also work for him.

From that point on, the Lieutenant and some of the other men started carrying tobacco and making offerings. In between the working, drinking, and playing, Dad would share with them how all beings have spirits. "No shit! everything?" they would ask. Dad would assure them that everything has a spirit and it offered them comfort. He told them that if they needed to, talk to a tree, a bush, a plant. Basically, anything connected to nature.

At one point, Dad was stationed at Danang Air Base as part of the Naval Support Activity Seabee unit. One evening, he and two buddies were walking to chow. They heard the whistling warning of an incoming attack. Dad heard a huge thud and the sound of metal ripping apart. All three men hit the deck. On either side of him, the other two men buckled up, groaning in pain. But Dad didn't have a single wound. Nothing. He shouted for the medics to come help his friends.

He never saw them again. He doesn't know if they lived or died.

The other men at the base who knew about Dad's tobacco ceremony talked about how it must have protected him. Dad certainly *felt* very protected.

Dad and the other Nett Lake boys seemed to run into each other all over Vietnam. Whether it was on a ship, in a bathroom in Danang, in the field—the little Bois Forte Reservation offered many young men to that war and, somehow, they always ran into each other.

One day, around noon, Dad's unit was getting ready to pull out on a mission. Dad heard someone call out to him and turned to see a dark face with grinning, white teeth that he recognized as Floyd Morrison from Nett Lake. Floyd was a few years younger than him, but they had known each other back home. Dad was so excited to see him that he got permission to stay back from the mission and spend time with Floyd.

They ate pizza, drank beer, played cards, and the other men even made space for him in a spare bunk. Floyd stayed with Dad for four days before returning to his base camp.

The next time they saw each other, Floyd was on his way home. After a night of drinking, Floyd woke up and headed to Danang Air Base to get on his flight home to the States. Instead, he was told that the flight had left a few hours before. He couldn't believe it. He was the only person Dad ever knew who missed his flight back home.

Floyd was so hungover, he decided he better not drink anymore until he caught the next flight home. He stayed right there at the R and R center to make sure he didn't miss the flight. He and Dad laugh about it today, remembering those moments. Floyd had ear injuries from being so close to the bombs, and he never returned to Vietnam, but he and Dad remained friends.

One of the ways the Nett Lake boys always found each other is that most of them were nicknamed "Chief" while on active duty. Ears perked up when anyone heard the words, "Hey, Chief!"

Another time, someone heard Dad's team call him "chief."

"We have a chief here, too," the man said. When Dad asked where he was from, the guide replied, "Minnesota." It turned out to be Hawk Connor, from Nett Lake. The two men were excited to see each other. Hawk took leave in order to accompany Dad back to base. When they arrived, the first thing his commanding officer said was "What the fuck am I gonna do with two blanket asses?" then he busted out laughing.

By this time in the military, Dad was used to being called things other than his name. He did not find it insulting. He usually didn't assign any judgement towards the speaker. Dad said the "soul brothers" called him Indian and he called them brothers. Only the white kids called them all Indian or Chief.

It didn't make them feel bad, though, it made them feel great. They felt proud to be an Indian "over there." Being a warrior comes naturally to Indians, and in a war zone, that garners respect. At home, being an Indian meant something else entirely.

Personally, I cannot even fathom this type of blatant racism in my military. I can't help but think that Dad shrugged it off because it was just how he was used to being treated. He didn't believe there was any other way *to* be treated.

His Lieutenant always called him Indian, not Chief like the rest of them. Dad said he was a super sharp man and he respected him greatly. When Dad needed to talk to him, he would say "Request permission to speak to the CC!"

"Speak, Indian," his Lieutenant would reply.

In the fall of 1969, while Dad was stationed at the Danang Air Base, a siren went off in the middle of the night. The base was being attacked. The men were jolted awake by the siren and quickly jumped from their bunks. As they pulled on their uniforms and grabbed their rifles, they could hear the rapid gunfire. The Marines had control of the situation, but Dad and the other men knew it was their duty to assist. By the time they got outside, the Viet Cong had cut the wired fencing and penetrated the base. The Marines, however, did have control of the situation. There were at least twenty Viet Cong bodies lying dead on the ground.

Dad and his fellow Seabees went back to their barracks. Most couldn't sleep, however, and ended up going to help with the bodies as soon as daylight arrived. As they worked, Dad discovered a familiar face lying among the dead. It was his on-base barber.

Dianna Good Sky

Even though he knew that the men and women of the Viet Cong often worked for the U.S. military during the day and fought for their cause at night, the sight of the barber's body affected him deeply. This was the same man who always greeted him with an exuberant "Oh! Hello there, my friend!" To which Dad would reply, "Hello there! How's my favorite barber today?"

As Dad stood there, chills went through his body. This barber used to shave him with a straight edge razor. This man, who was at the very least, very friendly to him, could have slit Dad's throat as he sat in the barber chair.

It took Dad a while to feel okay in a barber chair again. He still will not allow anyone to use a straight edge razor on him while he's in a barber's chair.

Dad spent fourteen months in Vietnam. When he returned home, physically intact, we got orders to Little Creek Base in Virginia. Another new beginning, in more ways than one. We would soon see that while Dad looked okay, he had changed.

9

VIRGINIA

I don't remember the actual move from Nett Lake to Norfolk, VA—I was in the third grade at the time. I do remember what a big change it was for our family. City life in Virginia was so different than it had been in San Francisco. Not only were we back in a city, but we also lived close to the ocean. I will never forget the first time I got a taste of the ocean (it tasted awful). Coming from calm lake water to ocean water with big waves is a big change.

We first rented a home in the Ocean View area of Norfolk. There, in a tiny two-bedroom duplex, we made great friends, even Mom and Dad had friends, and we could go outside to play. It was an easy commute to work for Dad, and if Mom needed the car, she could put us all in the car and take him to work.

Our attached neighbors in the duplex were Jack and Dorothy Allen. Mom and Dorothy became fast and lifelong friends. The men became fast drinking buddies.

Changes were happening fast. We were now able to be with Dad while he was in the military. He was often in uniform, and I was so proud of him. There is something inspiring about seeing your parent in uniform. Mom, as always, took excellent care of us, and Dad. This is when I started realizing that we had a certain pattern. Dad would go to work, Mom would clean and cook, and my sister and I went to school.

When Dad came home each day, we were so excited to see him. Then Lela and I would play outside until we were called in for dinner, and we would all sit down at the little table in the kitchen. Afterwards, we watched TV (it was the first time I saw The Wonderful World of Disney—which became a lifelong love of mine). Our little brother, Curtis, would get to pick what we watched. I would take my bath and then it was bedtime. Even though I didn't understand it at the time, that routine was very important to us. I know I loved it. It made me feel safe.

Then Friday nights would come. Usually, those nights were spent partying at our house or next door at the Allens's house. It was fun. The parents were less likely to pay attention to us and we could raise a little hell. Or eat snacks that we were not supposed to eat. This happened pretty much every Friday night.

We lived there for about a year or so and then, wonder of all wonders, my parents bought a house! It was a new build in Aragona Village in Virginia Beach. I asked Mom if Aragona Village was going to be like "The Village" at home. She laughed, hugged me and said, "No."

4729 Overman Ave is where we bonded even more as a family and were able to play a lot outside, play games, and even do cartwheels inside (if we didn't get caught). Mom cooked dinner every night, except on Sundays when we would usually get oatmeal, bacon, boiled eggs or pancakes and sausage, since it was Dad's turn to cook—and those were his favorites. My maternal grandpa came to live with us for a while. I remember us kids watching the three adults learning to square dance, decked out in their country clothes.

Mom's cousin, Bill Tibbetts, got stationed in Langley Air Force base while another cousin, Edwin Porter, was stationed in Oceana

Air base. We were surrounded by friends and family and it felt like people were always coming and going.

Dad started taking us to his work picnics with his Seabee unit. Wow, did those men know how to party! It was during the parties on the beach, or at the unit, that Mom chose to drive. She would always drive us there and then come pick us up. She didn't usually attend. Maybe she just wanted some alone time. I don't know. But I do know that my parents' drinking habits were starting to diverge. He drank more, she drank less.

Our routine at home, however, stayed the same, thanks to Mom. I later realized what a gift that was. Family dinners—and routine—were such a staple in our lives.

Often, Dad would bring a few of the younger members of his unit home for dinner, especially the ones with no family nearby. It was this that taught me the importance of helping others and sharing what we have, even if it isn't much. Mom never got upset, didn't even flinch when Dad showed up with these unexpected guests. He would walk in the door, usually Friday nights, and say, "Ar! We've got guests! Let's feed them a home cooked meal!"

The kids (I can say that now, but back then they were usually super cute older boys to me) would be so grateful and they'd express their gratitude to my mom and dad. Then, they'd sleep on the couch, or on the living room floor. The next day, Dad would take them back to the barracks on the Base.

In the midst of the fond childhood memories, there was also a shift that took place.

There was a noticeable difference in Dad's behavior on one particular night while we were eating dinner. We were having a normal family meal when there was suddenly a very loud "boom!" Dad's face immediately changed to fear and he jumped under the table! We had no idea what was going on. He stayed in a trance-like state for a few seconds, eyes glazed over. Then, as if he realized where he was, he got up, shook his head, and tried to smile at us, telling us that he was alright.

Dianna Good Sky

We must have been staring at him with saucer-like eyes, as round with fear and astonishment as his had been moments earlier.

My grandpa would laugh at him because he was a WWII Vet and knew exactly what was going on. Dad was suffering from PTSD. He tried to work through the stress by just being more aware of his surroundings. Sometimes he succeeded, other times he did not.

After that, Dad started closing all the curtains during dinner. I thought he was being mean because I wanted to see outside the window while we ate. If I opened the curtains, he would yell at me. I didn't understand it.

"People can see in and we are easy targets if they can see us," he said. As if that explained everything. I couldn't quite wrap my head around that concept. From that point on, the curtains had to be drawn during dinner at the kitchen table. Mom did not like it. But, I'm not sure what it was that she didn't like: keeping the curtains closed or watching her husband take a turn toward the demons that were obviously present somewhere in his world.

Of all the changes that happened during that time, however, I remember this the most: His drinking increased, and it was starting to affect our life as a family.

One thing that didn't change however, was our annual trip home to Minnesota for ricing season. It was a two-day drive from Virginia to Nett Lake. Dad would save up his "leave" days (I soon learned that "leave" meant vacation time for us) so that we could make that trip home during one of the most culturally significant and important times of year.

By that time, none of the family lived at Sugar Bush. Instead, the Goodsky land had become a vacation spot, a beautiful refuge for picnics and family barbecues. I loved it there, enjoying the food, swimming in the lake. We were a bunch of little Indians running around and it was a blast. It was a special place—probably because we always went there as a crowd, as a family. I loved playing with my cousins and the parents were often involved in our playful activity as well.

There *was* a lot of drinking at those family barbeques, but it really wasn't that big of a deal to me. Drinking was a normal occurrence when we were visiting the Rez, except on ricing days. Harvesting the beautiful grain remains an important part of our culture and heritage. It is such a special time, that even when we were all school-aged, we still went home every September for ricing season. We would start the year at Nett Lake Elementary in order to keep up with our schooling. The time of year was respected, so the high school kids—being old enough to rice— were always excused for ricing season.

Ricing season was a magical time for everyone. For the kids, it meant playing with the cousins all day outside in the beautiful September weather, with the leaves changing all around us. When the ricers came off the lake, we would run down to the lakeshore and help them get their rice to wherever we would be processing it that night. Supper was always very late, after a long day of ricing. The stories we would hear, the laughter, the games—it was a beautiful time.

We stayed at my maternal grandparents' house during the day, and most often parched and processed the rice at their house in the evening. While some adults did the ricing, others went duck hunting, but everyone worked together to gather, parch, jig, and fan the rice so that we all had enough to last a full year. Ricing season only lasts a few weeks, but when the families worked together, we could typically gather enough to make it last, and sometimes we'd have excess available to sell. I would bet that if you ask anyone in Nett Lake what their favorite memory is, ricing season would be at the top of the list. For many reasons. The biggest being the time you spend with the family. At the time, I didn't truly understand that this was also when I most fully experienced our culture.

One September afternoon, when I was still quite small, I went into my grandmother's house to get a drink of water because I had gotten thirsty playing "Auntie, auntie, I over" with my cousins. Inside, I smelled something really rancid and cautiously followed

Dianna Good Sky

the odor into the living room. There sat my grandma, my auntie Alice, auntie Lorraine, and my mom plucking the feathers off of ducks. They were using a lighter for part of the process, causing the awful smell. I remember thinking how awesome these ladies were that they could do that and feeling so grateful that I didn't have to. Yuck. Poor Ducks. But, oh how wonderful it was to eat fresh duck and wild rice soup. It was something we only got to eat while we were home in September.

It was on the weekends that the drinking commenced. The entire family would either go to the gravel pit for a picnic or Sugar Bush for a barbeque. That is where the adults really let themselves have a good time after such a long, laborious week.

If my grandma Jennie was there, no one dared drink when she was around. She and her sister, Auntie Alice, would often come to cook the bannock and salt pork, or any number of traditional dishes. They loved watching the kids play, and I suspect they also loved watching us enjoy their food. They wouldn't even get upset when our grubby hands reached into the cast iron skillet to pluck away pieces of thick, fruit-filled bread.

When the food was devoured, Grandma Jennie and Auntie Alice would head home on the pretense of exhaustion. It was after they left that the adults could bring out the beer.

While the parents drank, we would slide down the sandhills at the gravel pit or swim in the lake at Sugar Bush.

There was one year, while we were still in Virginia, that Dad, and Mom's cousin, Bill, drove home for ricing season on their own. Mom and the rest of us stayed in Virginia.

It was during this trip that Uncle Bill saw a side of Dad he had never seen before. Once they arrived in Nett Lake, they went their separate ways to be with their own families. Uncle Bill was staying with his brother, Gary. Just a few days after they had arrived, Bill heard someone pounding at Gary's front door. He got up to answer it and stood face-to-face with a side of my dad that still surprises him to this day. Dad's eyes were bloodshot, and his clothes were dirty and several days old. He was also carrying a rifle.

Warrior Spirit Rising

"Whoa, Gene. What are you doing?" Bill asked.

"I'm going to go take care of business over at the Conners'. I'm going to do what I was trained to do," Dad replied.

Bill stood there with his mouth open not quite sure what to say. "Why don't you come inside and rest a bit. Maybe have some coffee."

It was clear to Bill that Dad was super drunk, and very angry, and with that rifle in his hand, Bill was worried for him.

"No! I have to go do what I was trained to do!" Dad said.

After more attempts to get him in the house, Dad finally left. Bill and Gary held their breath that afternoon, waiting for the gun shots that, thankfully, never came.

Bill told Gary that all the time he had known Dad, even with all the card playing that they had done in Virginia with the wives, he'd never ever seen my dad like that.

It was so worrisome to Bill that he booked a flight home rather than take a chance and drive back to Virginia with Dad. That was a very good decision. He also decided it was best to pull away a bit from seeing him. It was hard, as he really enjoyed the time our families spent together. But he just couldn't get the visual of my dad—with his glazed, bloodshot eyes—out of his head.

Years later, Bill still remembers that day clearly. It is safe to say that this strange behavior was likely just one of the early indicators that Dad was struggling with PTSD from Vietnam. None of us had any idea what was happening to him, and I'm fairly certain that Dad had zero idea what was happening, either. Nor did he know how to deal with it. The drinking became his escape.

Dad drove back to Virginia by himself, oblivious to the reason that Bill didn't join him.

In time, Bill saw Dad again. He was still drinking. Bill just couldn't believe this was the same respectable, US Navy Seabee that he had shared so much time with in Virginia and on the twenty-eight-hour drive to Minnesota.

Dianna Good Sky

It wouldn't be the last time that people would pull away from Dad. But it was the last time that Dad went home to Nett Lake without us.

He was very late in returning home from that trip and Mom was really worried. She told me that he might get in big trouble with the military, something called AWOL, if he arrived home too late. He only had a certain number of days he could be gone.

Once he returned, I asked him if he got into trouble and he said just a little, but it was not for me to worry about. Everything was going to be fine. I believed him. Or, I wanted to.

Our routine went back into place shortly after he returned. But the changes with Dad and his drinking were starting to come faster.

A missed dinner.

No desire to play catch in the yard.

Mom crying more often.

When we misbehaved, Mom used to threaten us with punishment from Dad—you know, "Stay in your room until your dad comes home, he's going to deal with you!" At that point, however, she was doing more of the disciplining herself.

The Navy was very forgiving of Dad's drinking. Once his drinking got worse, there were days that they would send him home, early, to "sleep it off." I remember thinking that the Navy was pretty nice to let him come home in the mornings so he could nap. But Mom didn't like it, I could tell. She was very worried about our situation. I understand this. He was the breadwinner. She thought about getting a job, but with only one car, and with dad's increasingly unreliable behavior, she didn't. She was very stressed. I could feel it. Not only that, but I frequently caught her crying, as much as she tried to hide it.

Then came the moments I hated the most.

Sometimes, when Dad came home drunk, he insisted on teaching us our heritage. I'm not sure what came over him in those moments. Looking back, it was almost as though the excess alcohol prompted him to grasp at his life's unfulfilled purpose.

He came into our bedrooms and woke us up in loud, drunken tones. He yelled at us to get up so he could "Teach us how to be an Indian." My brother, sister, and I dragged ourselves out of bed, straining to keep our eyes open, exhausted, angry, and a little scared.

Dad made us sit in a row on the couch as he tried to teach us Indian words. But it was the middle of the night and I had no desire to listen to this drunk Indian teach *me* how to speak. Besides, his words sounded like gibberish. *What was he even saying?* I hated it.

I am pretty sure we all hated it.

And then, as if the language lessons weren't enough, he turned on Pow Wow music and forced us to dance Indian.

When I say force, I mean that he made us all stand up and move our feet, and then, because we were not in time with the music, he yelled at us for doing it wrong. He demonstrated it himself, even in his drunkenness. He insisted he was keeping time with the drumbeat.

When he got loud—particularly during the dancing—Mom would wake up. Thank goodness! Seeing her come in the room was like watching your knight in shining armor show up just before you're beheaded.

She tried to be gentle with him and he got argumentative. "Let me make you coffee," she would say. Dad could never turn down a cup of coffee.

Dad always sipped his coffee in deep concentration, focused on only one thing: passing his knowledge on to his children. Within a few minutes, however, he would begin to slouch, and his eyes would droop. Instead of sobering him, the coffee somehow slowed him down. It was only later that I realized Mom put Nyquil in the coffee. We all came to hope that he would drink it quickly so he would pass out. Thank you, Mom, for saving us.

As Dad drifted into sleep, Mom would usher the three of us back to bed. Relieved, we went into our rooms and fell back into a restless slumber, half-dreaming in Ojibwe, drums beating the

Dianna Good Sky

same rhythm as our hearts. It was a miserable way to spend the night and getting up for school the next day was always hard.

I came to hate those nights, and I didn't like how he seemed to only do this when he was drunk. No one wants to learn from a drunk. It would take many years for me to finally embrace our history and desire to learn our language.

Aside from the nightly cultural lessons, the other big change during that season happened at Christmas. Prior to the drinking, which Dad used to do only occasionally or just on the weekends, the holidays were pretty good. I never felt like we were missing anything, and Mom always gave us spending money so we could buy gifts for each other, or we did chores to earn a little bit of money to buy gifts for the family. She did a great job teaching us how to make Christmas beautiful. It was her favorite holiday.

Mom was also the best gift wrapper ever. Her wrapping was precise, and she taught us how to wrap properly. She would make these beautiful bows, too, or use ribbon. She taught us that by making the packaging beautiful, we make gift giving beautiful.

That Christmas, however, changed my outlook for the rest of my life.

The first thing I noticed that year was that Mom never offered us opportunities to earn money for gifts. She also didn't give us money to buy gifts. When pressed, she confided that Christmas was going to be very different. When I asked her why, she told me, bluntly, that we didn't have enough money that year to do much. She also told us that she was sorry, so very sorry. We would not be getting very many gifts that year.

I was a little surprised, and even though I noticed that Dad's drinking had become worse and worse, I guess I just never realized the full scope of how his drinking impacted us until that moment.

I felt bad for my little brother and sister. They seemed too young to notice, but they were also too young to have to miss out on a great Christmas morning. I talked to my mom and asked her what I could do for the kids. She advised me to make them something homemade. I used the skills she taught me as a present wrapper to make them gifts just as pretty as Mom's. I was very proud of that. Even though money was, apparently, nonexistent, Mom still insisted on making the packages as beautiful as ever. The only thing inside the wrapping, however, was a new hat and mittens.

We also had a very lean Christmas dinner. But Mom made the best of it. She was good at making the best of bad situations.

Getting on the school bus after Christmas that year was something that I still remember to this day. I was in the fifth grade. I knew everybody would be bragging about their Christmas gifts and what they received. I didn't want to talk about my Christmas or the lack of presents, so I crouched down in the seat with my arms around my knees and my head down on my arms, in hiding. When pushed by my friends to tell them what I got for Christmas, I just told them I didn't feel good.

I was utterly embarrassed. I was too young to articulate that what I received was a deeper understanding of gift giving, no matter what was inside the box (especially if the boxes were wrapped beautifully). Instead, I just slouched in my seat, humiliated.

I prayed the bus would hurry up and get to the school so I could escape my own embarrassment, and the terrifying feeling that I would be found out. No one could know that I only received a hat and mittens for Christmas. I don't think there was a day until then, and after, that I was so grateful to see the school. I bolted off that bus. I still recall that feeling. I made a huge decision that day— I would never allow my kids to experience that level of humiliation or embarrassment about their Christmas. I kept that promise to my children.

I received a promise from Mom that Christmas, as well. She promised me that she would make things better. I had no idea what she could do, but I believed her. I heard something in her voice that made me not think twice about her meaning. She was my knight in shining armor, she promised.

Dianna Good Sky

10
PAYDAY

Not long after Christmas, Mom went out and got her first job. She had no experience, and no training. She and Dorothy, her friend from Ocean View, were experiencing the same things at home. The men of the house were drinking most of the money, so the women decided to step in and do something different. So, they both got jobs—with zero experience and no cars—at a mushroom canning facility.

They carpooled to work, taking turns driving their spouses to work so they could use the car. It worked for a while, but then they started having trouble getting the cars. They lost their jobs because they couldn't get to their shifts. Mom was deflated. But me? Well, I didn't like her working. Our little routine was disrupted every time she went to work because she was no longer always there for us. I was secretly glad when she lost her job. I'm ashamed to admit that, but our world was spiraling, and I craved normalcy.

Dad was drinking more and more, and the effect was creeping into our everyday lives. Money was scarce, and not just on holidays.

Back then, the military payday was every two weeks on a Friday. Most Friday nights, we didn't know what to expect. Would Dad come home with money so we could go to the grocery store? At that point, I knew that we were living paycheck to paycheck. That much was clear. Prior to all the drinking, I never noticed the cupboards going bare. As the drinking increased, both the cupboards and the refrigerator slowly became more and more sparse, until they were empty. Empty of food, at least. We had staples such as ketchup, mustard, and Miracle Whip, but there was nothing else.

One Friday, I went to get a snack and opened the cupboards to find a single can of tomato paste. That was frightening. I knew that things were bad, and they were only getting worse.

That Friday we kept asking Mom when we were going to eat. We sat together at the dining room table, waiting. I opened the fridge and there was nothing there. I opened the cupboard again. Still just one can of tomato paste. I sat back down with Mom and my sister and brother and we talked and visited, trying to distract each other through the waiting. Dad didn't come home with the paycheck.

As time went on, Mom admitted that there wouldn't be any groceries that night. More time passed. We still waited there at the table, even though she told us to go play in our rooms or watch TV. Eventually the younger kids got up and left the room, but mom simply sat there, and I stayed with her.

That was the first night I asked her why she stayed.

"Where would we go?" She said. "I can't get a good job; I don't have a car. I don't know how I would take care of you kids by myself."

The feeling of defeat and resignation was strong that evening.

My thoughts turned from food to my Dad. How drunk would he be when he got home? Would we be asleep? Would he wake

Dianna Good Sky

us up? Would we have to try to dance and speak Indian and get yelled at again? The hunger pains subsided as I prayed in earnest that he would just come home and go to sleep.

I went to the refrigerator again, as if food would magically appear, but also trying to figure out what kind of dinner we could come up with using what we had. As I stared into the empty fridge, I made another promise to myself: My children will never have to see an empty fridge or cupboard. Ever.

I started escaping our house more often and spent a lot of time at my best friend's house. Once, she asked me to get something out of the refrigerator for her and when I opened it, it was full of food. I actually got jealous. I wished with my entire being that we had a fridge full of food.

Mom helped me understand that sometimes Dad drank the whole paycheck. It was then that she had to borrow money. Thank goodness for Dorothy Allen and their mutual situations. Dorothy and Mom took turns helping each other out. They provided each other with a shoulder to cry on, they would make each other laugh, and when things were particularly tough, they shared money and food when their husbands drank the paychecks away. Ah, girlfriends. To this day, it is one of the most cherished relationships that I have. Thank you, mom and Dorothy, for teaching me this.

There were a few instances where the drinking got so bad that Dad would say he was going to stop drinking. I am sure this was at my mom's insistence. He would go to treatment, and things would be better for a bit.

One time, I was so hopeful that he had finally quit forever. There was food in the house again and Mom and Dad decided to paint our bedroom and get us new sheets and bedding! I chose purple. We compromised with lilac. Mom told me I got to choose because I was the oldest, even though I shared the room with my sister (and sometimes our brother if we had family living with us, which happened frequently).

My hope was short-lived—Dad came home drunk. Again. This pattern happened at least twice while we lived at 4729 Overman Ave.

We endured Virginia together, all four of us. We each had our share of troubles while dealing with our drunk dad. But we were children and Mom was stuck, for our sakes.

I threw myself into my studies at school and always got good grades. I hadn't yet discovered reading as an escape, but I liked *Teen* magazine and listening to Donny Osmond. They were a nice escape from my reality. But at that time, things got so bad that I didn't want to be a part of it anymore. I wanted to get the hell out of Dodge.

I decided to run away.

I laid in my bed next to my sister—she and I were sharing a full bed at this point—thinking about how to run away. I stared at the little window in the corner intently, wondering if I could get up there and also, would I fit? I decided that, yes, I could climb out the window. When I thought about where to go, I decided that I really didn't care. Any place was better than home. Maybe I could go to Sonya's house. They always had food and their dad didn't drink. It would be so much better than here.

Suddenly, my little sister asked me a question and jolted me out of my beautiful thoughts of Sonya's full refrigerator. I told her to be quiet and go to sleep, but she pressed on. I finally told her that I was going to run away. I hated it here.

Her beautiful, little face looked up at me from her pillow.

She draped her little arm around my belly.

"Can I go with you?" She said. And she looked so sad, pitiful almost.

"No"

"Why not?"

"I can't take care of you." I was not sure how I was going to take care of myself, so there was no way I could take care of her, too.

Dianna Good Sky

She told me she could take care of herself. She promised she could.

I looked at her small face and I told her that she was too little to do that. Mom would take care of her.

She moved closer to me and looked at me intently with her beautiful brown eyes. "But I don't want you to go. I don't want to be here without you. I would miss you too much. I love you." Then she hugged me tighter.

What can I say? I couldn't help but feel a tremendous amount of love for this baby girl lying next to me and I realized in that instant that I could never leave home because I could never leave her. I snuggled back into bed and hugged her tightly, telling her I would not leave and that I loved her so much, too. We fell asleep tightly wrapped in each other's arms. I was eleven years old.

11
LOSING EVERYTHING

I knew we wouldn't be in Virginia forever. Being in the military, you are subject to moving often. I was able to adapt well to the moves, frankly, because I had so much shit going on at home. And, I think most military children adapt well to change. At least, they do it often enough that it becomes their norm.

Eventually, Dad got orders to Great Lakes, Illinois, just outside of Chicago. Not only that, but he also took leave in between duty stations, which meant a trip home to Minnesota.

I was so happy to be around family! I also knew that Dad wouldn't bother us because he would be drinking with his friends and avoiding Grandma Jennie's house. What a relief. I looked forward to playing with the cousins, not worrying about food, and being surrounded by family and love.

It was while we were in Minnesota that Mom decided to leave Dad. At least, it was the first time she decided to leave him.

The next few months were complicated.

We ended up in Brackett, Wisconsin, in a trailer park about ten miles outside of Eau Claire. Mom told me it was close enough to home, yet far enough away to not actually be there. She explained that it was also close enough to Dad in Great Lakes, just in case he ever wanted to visit. I blew that idea off quickly. I didn't want him to visit.

What I really wanted was to live in Nett Lake. If we were going to leave Dad, there was huge comfort for me back home. Why couldn't we stay? But it wasn't just proximity to Dad or distance from home that took us to Wisconsin. It was because Mom chose to leave with another man, and because of who she chose, we had to be away from Nett Lake.

I hated her choice. I wanted us to be by ourselves. My respect for my mom changed at that point. I was a pre-teen and strong-willed, and I certainly wasn't afraid to tell her how much I hated what she did. It's ironic, isn't it? I wanted so bad for her to leave Dad, and when she did, I hated that situation, too.

I had no problem voicing my opinion and wanted to drive the man away. I gave no thought to anything else except that he didn't belong with us. He only lasted a few weeks.

Unfortunately, he took his car with him. We were left in a trailer park, ten miles from the nearest big town, in the middle of farmland Wisconsin, with no vehicle. I told Mom we'd be fine.

It was 1973 and I was just starting seventh grade. Mom applied for jobs and also applied for welfare. I loved this new life now. It was just us and I never had to worry about food, or drunk talks, or fights from my parents' bedroom, but after only a few months, Mom sat me down and told me she just couldn't do it anymore. She couldn't get hired and there wasn't enough money to live. She couldn't take care of us and her job was to make sure we were taken care of.

Then she dropped a bomb.

She and Dad had been talking. Dad promised, again, to quit drinking and this time, she assured me that he was serious. She would make sure that he kept his promise and that we would never have to return to the kind of life we had in Virginia.

I was mad. Very mad.

She asked me if I would at least be open to a visit from him. Just to see for myself how he had changed. He missed us, she said, so much so that he quit drinking, and he wanted to be with us. She sounded confident. I think, really, she was just hopeful. She knew he would take care of us this time.

He came for a visit. I was reluctant, but he was sober. He apologized to us and promised us he was done drinking forever. And, not for the first time, I believed him.

We moved to Great Lakes, Illinois to be with Dad. It was an interesting move. Mom left me and my sister behind in Wisconsin for a week or so while we finished out the term at school. She and my brother drove to Illinois to start unpacking and get settled in our new (to us) home. Lela and I stayed with friends (we had, at least, made friends there—good people—in Brackett, Wisconsin) who then put us on a bus to Great Lakes.

It was 1973. I was twelve years old and my sister was nine. Can you even imagine? Just two girls on a six-hour bus ride by themselves. Of course, Mom and Dad gave me specific instructions on how to act, how to take care of Lela and most exciting—I got spending money! We bought candy. What can I say?

To my surprise and happiness, Dad kept his promise. At first, I waited with anticipation for the shit to hit the fan again. It didn't. Soon, we were back to a full fridge and cupboards. There was a sense of normalcy that I was so grateful for. We were even able to take regular shopping trips every Saturday following payday.

Life seemed pretty good. We sat together at the dinner table every night and I even noticed that Mom added Pillsbury croissants to the menu sometimes, instead of the usual bread slices. I was so happy to see that things were, in fact, getting better. Our little family was together again. Dad would come home every night

Dianna Good Sky

from work and we would practically knock him down with our joy in seeing him come through the door. After the hugs and enthusiastic welcome, he would sit in his recliner and we would help him remove his boots and put his slippers on. It was so heavenly having our family be the family I knew we really were, without the drinking. Laughter had returned, food was plentiful, and we were all very happy.

Then, I woke up one morning and noticed that there wasn't the usual smell of breakfast cooking. I wondered why. I got ready for school and started to head downstairs when Mom came out of the bedroom on the opposite end of the hall and I caught sight of something on her face. As she approached me, she told me to go on down the stairs. I went ahead, but I looked back at her. Something was wrong.

She had a black eye.

My mind raced. *How could that happen? Where did she go last night?* Nowhere, she had stayed home. *Who was here?* No one besides the family. *Oh my gosh,* I thought, *Did Dad hit her? He must have!* I became suddenly, shockingly angry.

Have you ever seen your mother with a black eye? Knowing that it was your father that did that to her?

If you have, I'm sorry. I know how painful that is

When she came downstairs, I confronted her. "What happened?" I demanded.

"Never mind." She said. "I'm okay, nothing to worry about."

She refused to talk about it. I tried to press her for answers even though I knew the truth of the matter, she assured me that she was ok. I told her we had to leave. She told me to be quiet and get ready for school. She apologized for not cooking breakfast. I told her I didn't care about breakfast. I wanted to stay home with her. She told me the best thing I could do for her was to carry on as normal as possible.

My first thought was that maybe he should go back to drinking. Even if we had to get up in the middle of the night and listen to him try to teach us how to be an Indian, at least he wouldn't be hitting Mom!

If this was his replacement for drinking, I would put up with whatever I needed to put up with as long as he didn't touch her again. I knew I could protect the rest of them from the crap we had to put up with. I was old enough to babysit for others and from then on, I knew I would save my money so that we could have food, if and when he didn't bring the money home. I'd do anything to keep him from hitting her again.

Just in case, I started sleeping with a knife under my pillow.

It wasn't until years later that I learned the truth about my mom's black eye. It wasn't alcohol or domestic abuse. Instead, it was something much simpler. Something that no one seemed to talk about or deal with in those days.

The night Dad hit her was a normal night for us all. There were no significant events that he could recall, but he started dreaming.

Dad dreamt that he was in the jungle of Vietnam. He was by himself, away from the base, but being chased by the Viet Cong. They ran after him and he was running and running until he finally felt that he had outrun them. Then there was a woman standing in front of him, saying something in Vietnamese. He could barely hear her, but her voice became louder as she approached him. He had to get her out of the way, so he started throwing punches.

"Gene! Gene! You punched me! Wake up! Wake up!" Mom had shouted at him, desperate.

He finally woke up to see my mom standing there, holding her eye. Slowly, he began to realize what he had done.

The PTSD proved to be stronger than sobriety, and soon after this, Dad started drinking again. Alcohol's grip on him became so strong, that he would even show up to work hungover, if not completely hammered. The Navy used to deal with this by sending him home to recover. His addiction had a vice grip on him.

As strange as it sounds, I was relieved. At least when he was drinking, he never hit her. I had babysitting money saved, I knew we could endure. I didn't like it, but I was comforted by that fact.

Dianna Good Sky

Since, at the time, I didn't know why he had hit her, I made a logical connection in my young mind: he was sober when he hit her, so he must have been mad at her for keeping him from drinking. I think it was normal for my twelve-year-old brain to make up a story, any story, to make sense of things.

This round of drinking was a bit different. Somehow, we never ran out of food, we never had a bad Christmas (relatively speaking, of course) and Mom always found a way to make things seem ok. Dad was also not binge drinking on paydays. Instead, he would drink more often. He would sometimes come home early in the morning, still in uniform, as I was getting ready to go to school. I would be so happy that he was no longer waking us up in the middle of the night.

I noticed, however, that my parents argued more often. No hitting, but more yelling. Let me be clear: Dad was yelling at Mom; she was taking it. I hated it. And I held my breath as I waited for him to hit her. I knew that if he did, I would not stand for it. I used to imagine storming the bedroom door and attacking him and saving her. Like she had saved me, us really, so many times before. I knew I could take him and his drunk ass.

I was not happy there, but by that time, I had figured out that I could escape in books. So I did. I would get so engrossed in them that he would yell at me when I couldn't hear him trying to get my attention. If you've ever heard my dad yell, well, let's just say that it's not very pleasant. Soon, he forbade me from reading downstairs. I had to do it in my room. Fine with me.

I had a tough time in Illinois. Things were not good at home, and so, unlike my foiled attempt to run away from home in Virginia, this time I actually followed through with it. One day after school, I decided that I would rather go to my friend's house than go home. This was North Chicago, Illinois, so not exactly the safety net of the Village. But I thought I could just tell my parents I missed the bus and had to catch my best friend, Karen's bus instead. I knew her dad would give me a ride home; he was a nice dad. I was wrong about so many things that day!

Warrior Spirit Rising

Karen's parents weren't home when we got off the bus. When I tried to call our house, no one answered. Then, my boyfriend, Dan, happened to come and visit me and I lost *all* track of time. The next thing I knew, Dad was pulling into Karen's driveway. I was jolted back into reality. He was livid! Once in the car, he asked me a question. "I missed the bus," I remember saying, and WHAM! He slapped me across the face so hard that I saw stars. I knew my friends saw him do that and I was beyond humiliated. Once home, he banished me to my room, and I was so very glad to go. I cried and I cried, mostly from embarrassment.

I ran away that night. It's funny to me now, but I only got as far as the house just around the corner. I had seventeen dollars of babysitting money (I could have sworn that I had at least $100, but oh well) and nowhere to go. Not far from us lived a girl named Joyce. She was a very cool, laid back, always skipping school kind of girl who was a grade ahead of me at North Chicago Jr High. We had never spoken, but she always smiled at me when I smiled at her.

So, I snuck out of the house and found myself knocking on her door at 10 p.m. Her mom answered and I must have looked pretty crazy standing there. Joyce came outside and I told her what happened, and I begged her to let me spend the night with her. She made up a lie (which seemed rather easy for her to do, I noticed) and told her parents that my parents had gone out of town and they thought that I would be okay by myself, but I was scared and I had to spend the night with her now. They were all so kind and I never forgot their graciousness. I wished my parents were that nice. But shit, if my dad didn't believe that I missed the bus, there was no way in hell he would believe some sob story about a girl being left alone. Oh well.

I was still at Joyce's house the next day when the military cops came and picked me up around 1 p.m. Apparently, my parents had made a report to the base police (we were living in military housing at the time) and the military cops had grilled all the kids on the bus. Joyce crumbled. I didn't blame her for anything. Anyway, I

Dianna Good Sky

realized I had no clean underwear. I was ready to go home and face the music.

Surprisingly, Dad was very remorseful and even apologized to me. We got along okay for a little while. I graduated from eighth grade, and my parents even surprised me with a graduation dress that I never thought they could afford.

But as time passed, Dad's drinking picked up again. He went into treatment, but I'd lost count of how many times he had attempted that ruse. It never helped him. I knew he'd be a drunk forever.

12
TOWN DRUNK
1976

In 1976, Dad got orders to Puerto Rico. We happily left Great Lakes and went on our usual family "furlough" to Minnesota. Home. I could not wait.

While Mom took the rest of us to Nett Lake, Dad went to Mississippi for some special training.

I was so relieved to have a break from the craziness. A break from the constant worry about what exactly was going to happen when Dad came home drunk.

It was while we were in Nett Lake that I started telling my mom, again, to leave him. Together we could do it, I told her. We didn't need anyone else. It was better for all of us to not be with him. If he could be sober, sure, keep him around. But he was never able to stay sober, so we were better off without him.

To my surprise and utter joy, Mom chose to leave him, again, and stay in Minnesota.

Dad did not take the news very well. He was still in school in Mississippi when Mom spoke to him, and he hadn't yet executed his re-enlistment in the Navy. We thought Dad would carry on in his drunk, Navy life. We were wrong. He decided he was done and convinced himself that he couldn't carry on in the military without his family. He asked the clerk in the dispersing office how much child support he would have to pay once the divorce was finalized. They told him that he'd have to pay 75% of each paycheck to my mom. That was a total crock of shit, but he believed them, and he knew he couldn't live on that. But seriously, who could? Based on that bad advice and feeling like a failure as a father and husband, he decided to get out of the Navy with just eight years to retirement. Alcoholism will do that.

Ah, shit. What was this going to mean? I dreaded Mom getting back with him, but I didn't need to worry. The truth is, Mom kind of went crazy with her newfound freedom, and before long, I knew they wouldn't ever get back together.

There were no houses available for us, but we finally settled in an old home just outside of the Village. Effie Day's old house. It had electricity with no running water, but I did not care that we had to use a slop pail and an outhouse again. I did not care one bit! I was fourteen years old and I was thrilled, even though that outhouse was old and stunk to high heaven.

Mom found a job right away and I was so very proud of her. Her job required her to travel and she was able to buy nice clothes for her trips and work meetings. I thought she was so beautiful and smart! My knight in shining armor, in spite of her flaws. For the first time in ages, we had no hunger pains. And while the responsibility of the younger kids fell on me while Mom worked, I was happy to do it—most days. We did fine. She used to buy us canned goods to keep meal prep easy since I had a very busy high school schedule. I was in the ninth grade and loving every moment of being home and being active in school. Life was very good.

Dad eventually came home too, to Nett Lake. He moved in with his mom, my Grandma Gamaht.

If I thought his drinking was bad before, I was ill-prepared for what happened next.

The first time we saw him was soon after he got out of the Navy, when he came over to our house. It was uncomfortable for me, but my brother, Curtis, was very happy to see him, at least at first. Lela was guarded. Which is understandable. Mom was a little on edge, herself.

Dad started crying while he was there with us, and I recall feeling a bit sad for him as memories of what a beautiful family we used to be—in houses with running water—flooded through me. But I also felt resentful. This was all his fault. We shouldn't have to be living apart. We should be living in a nice house, with running water, and eating dinner at the dinner table every evening instead of sitting on the couch eating in the living room because Mom was at work. We should be going shopping on the weekends as a family, and Mom and Dad should be together; sober and happy. It's all his fault.

As soon as Mom realized that Dad's display of emotion was making us feel bad, she told him to leave and to come back when he could just visit.

The next time he came to the house, he was drunk.

I mean, drunker than I'd ever seen him before. The kind of drunk that makes you wonder, *what happened to this man?* He clearly hadn't showered in a while. Yuck. When he hugged us and tried to kiss us, we couldn't turn our heads away fast enough. Mom didn't let him stay, she told him he was not allowed to see us while he was drinking. I was so glad she told him that.

We never went to visit him. We never knew what we would find if we did. But since he lived in the Village, I would occasionally see him walking around on the dirt roads. I always avoided him.

It didn't take long for the other kids to see an opportunity. They began teasing me about my drunk, stinking, Dad. I was humiliated. Again.

Even though we did not seek him out, he tried to visit us, especially if he knew Mom wasn't home. She had chased him away a few times before he realized he should try when she wasn't around. I guess he looked for her car to be sure before he knocked on the door.

The first few times he came around, we let him in the house. He was our Dad, after all. And frankly, they raised us to be respectful of our elders. But we soon realized what a mistake it was to let him in. Screw what we knew we were supposed to do!

From then on, when we realized it was him at the door, we would hide. Usually under the bed, just in case he somehow made it into the house. I remember getting as far back away from the edge of the bed, as close to the wall as possible. Holding my breath and praying for him to leave. Lela, Curtis, and I were stone cold silent until we felt sure he was gone.

Every single time this happened, I made an even firmer commitment to stay away from him. Forget asking him to come to my volleyball or softball games, the Christmas choir recital, or even the boys basketball games where I was a pom-pom girl. Forget all of that. Mom was there for me and I was happy with that. As far as I was concerned, Dad was an embarrassment and I wanted nothing to do with him. But I missed my nuclear family. I missed being a part of something special, where you knew you were surrounded by love and joy with no worries about running into your drunk dad.

I decided I would make my own family.

I was fifteen and had just started the tenth grade at Orr High School. I carefully chose the father of my baby-to-be and I asked him to get me pregnant. He was eighteen. It didn't take long.

Telling my Mom was hard, but doable. This was my decision, after all. We had a practical, woman-to-woman discussion, and she just said, "Well, don't expect me to babysit for you." Ok, then.

But holy hell, talking to my Dad? I had zero intention of telling him and I was going to make every effort to avoid him. Absolutely. I mean, by this time, he was so broken and drunk that sometimes he would be smelling like alcohol, stinking of no shower, *and* be all pissy, and he would be in public places, asking for money. No way did I want to talk to him about it.

Mom came home from work one day and said, "Well, Dianna, at least you getting pregnant is going to do us all a bit of good. They decided that a pregnant girl can't be in a house with no running water, so they gave us a house in Pine View."

All I could think about was how excited I was to have running water again. And, because I was so young, I also felt somewhat smug. "HMMMPFH..See! Me being pregnant isn't all the bad!"

We moved into the house next to our Uncle Skunko, Mom's brother. He was raising his three kids on his own (one was special needs) and he was a great musician (like most on that side of the family). We liked living there. As my pregnancy progressed, I couldn't handle school and even though I was a straight-A student, I dropped out. I seriously thought—as I had promised my mom—that I could handle it all: school, baby, activities—by myself.

By that time, I had broken up with the baby's father even though he wanted to marry me. Marry? No, I wanted a baby, not a husband. I dropped out of high school in full confidence that after I gave birth, I would resume my life as normal and then join the Navy, something I had wanted to do from the time I was twelve years old.

It was very early one morning—I was eight months pregnant—when I woke up to a knock at the door. I had fallen asleep on the couch the night before. *It's so early*, I thought. And then I froze. *Oh shit.* It was Dad.

I debated whether to simply hold my breath until he left or answer the door, so he didn't wake everyone else in the house.

He kept knocking. I think he heard the TV.

I finally got up and let his stinky ass in the house, and then crawled back onto the couch. I was fairly small for being eight months pregnant—I had been on a diet for the past two months—and I was hoping he wouldn't see me.

He sat down on the couch, next to me. *Dang it.* Then he proceeded to talk and talk for what seemed like forever. It seemed

Dianna Good Sky

like forever, because soon after he started talking to me, my water broke!

There was no way in hell I was going to tell him what was happening. I knew he would want to come to the hospital, and there was *absolutely* no way in hell I wanted him in the hospital.

He (finally!) put his hand on my tiny belly and told me that even though I was pregnant, he was proud of me. Thanks, Dad. Now get out. But what I actually said was that I really needed to use the bathroom. I was so relieved when he left.

I gave birth that day via C-section. It was May 13, 1977.

When Dad came around to see my son, I let him, and of course, he cried. By this time, none of us wanted him to be around, however, so I made up an excuse so that he would have to leave.

This avoidance continued for all of us.

Sometimes we would be forced to see him, usually by accident or because he sought us out. Lela recalls how one time, he asked her for money, and she happened to have $7, so she gave it to him. She remembers thinking how sad she was that he was taking money from her, how stinky he was, and how she knew she'd never get the money back (you owe Lela $7, Dad).

And yet, we couldn't avoid hearing about how bad he was doing. He only seemed to be getting worse. By then, we had given up on him.

13
DREAM OF THE LIGHT
1978

You sometimes hear people say that life is filled with coincidences. Well, for us, we call those spiritual messages. Dad's life has been marked by spiritual messages.

They always came at unexpected moments: his grandfather's charcoal, his increased passion for nature, the porcupine escaping its box. He was heavily in the throes of drinking and living a life that was unrecognizable, even to him, when another spiritual message marked his life.

He dreamt that night, but in his dream there was only darkness. It was pitch black and he couldn't see anything, not even his hand in front of his face. He was afraid. He felt lost and isolated. When he tried to see what was around him, there was no relief from the darkness. And he couldn't find his way out.

He tried to walk but that didn't seem to be working—he kept tripping over rocks in his path. Instead, he decided to run as his fear escalated. The rocks kept tripping him and he kept running into trees, which just increased his fears.

After what seemed like a very long time, with fear firmly embedded in his mind and the darkness still surrounding him, he gave up. He dropped to his knees and cried. From that place, on his hands and knees, he hollered, "Somebody, help me! Somebody, help me!" He kept hollering.

He felt miserable and lost. He started pounding his fist on the ground, angry that nobody was helping him. Angry that he couldn't find his way out. But he kept screaming. What else could he do?

"Somebody, help me." This time his voice came out as a whisper. He was going to give up the fight. He wanted this to end. He wanted this hopeless, miserable feeling to go away. He didn't want to feel like this anymore.

He stopped pounding his fist and he sat up.

When he finally lifted his head in resignation, he saw a light in the distance. The light was small, like it was very far off.

He stared at it.

He watched it because it was the only thing he could see. It was still pitch black all around him, except for that tiny pinprick of light.

Finally, this light begins approaching him and he understands. He's suddenly not afraid at all. He understands that there's nothing to be afraid of by looking at this light.

Out of the light came the form of a spirit. It had no features on its face, only long white hair and light all around. As he watched, the spirit reached out and handed him a torch. As soon as Dad took the torch, the spirit disappeared.

It was only later that Dad realized that the spirit was his Grandpa Burnside.

With the torch in his hand, he was suddenly able to stand and start walking through the woods. When he got through the woods, he couldn't see what was there, but he knew that the woods' edge was right in front of him.

As soon as he stepped out of the woods, he woke up.

The dream was so real that Dad never forgot it. Nor did he forget the horrible sensation of being lost and alone in the darkness. His waking life was not much different. Dad went right back to drinking. He wanted to drown his hopelessness.

Dianna Good Sky

14

DEATH AND LIFE
1980

I left for the Navy on January 16th, 1980. I only told my Dad I was leaving when I ran into him by accident at Glendale. He promised to get sober.

By March, Dad was still drinking heavily. The Minnesota winter was in full force that year. There was plenty of snow on the ground and the outside temperature was below freezing. It was not unusual for the end of winter in Nett Lake, but definitely a reason to stay inside. That was not why Dad was drinking, though. This was just another binge drinking episode. But this time, something was different.

Dad started to feel the effects of some illness. He wasn't sure what came over him, but he was feeling sick, really sick. After three straight days of drinking with little to no sleep (at least he doesn't remember whether he slept or not), Dad finally told his drinking buddies to leave so that he could lie down. He was feeling too awful to continue partying. His buddies didn't like that he was kicking them out, but he knew he had to rest. He had to do something to feel better.

They slowly, finally, made their way out. Dad looked around as he contemplated where to rest. His tiny apartment in the Elderly Unit— I affectionately call it "The Wrinkle Ranch"—was filthy. He couldn't deal with it, though. He went into the bathroom and looked into the mirror. He saw the reflection and didn't recognize that person.

"Who the f*** are you?"

As he saw his lips move in the mirror, he knew it had to be him. He blinked a few times, even tried washing his face, even though the motion of bending over did not feel very good at all. But he wanted, maybe even needed, to find himself in that reflection. He wanted very much for the reflection to change. But, no matter how hard he stared into that mirror, the reflection just kept looking worse and worse. He was disgusted. On top of feeling so sick physically, he just couldn't help but feel lousy thinking how awful his life was at that moment. Finally, he turned away from the disgusting reflection. He couldn't look at himself any longer.

He had to lie down.

He wanted to die.

He was just too miserable.

Dad left the bathroom and looked over at the tiny table in the eating area next to the small, galley kitchen and saw the bottle of Vodka—three-quarters full—sitting on that table, looking so innocent. He had a brief, but major, moment of reflection. *I was once an honorable man.* He thought to himself. *And now I can't even stand up. How did I get here?*

He turned and went into the bedroom, weak and miserable. He laid down on the homemade quilt on his twin bed and hoped that sleep, or death, would take him quickly.

On one hand, it seemed that sleep would never come. He felt so terrible that all he could think about was how he wished he could feel better. On the other hand, it seemed as if sleep came instantly.

He was only asleep for a very short time when he woke quite suddenly.

Dianna Good Sky

He was feeling one hundred percent better. Somehow his short rest had cured him of all his ills in an instant. He was surprised that he felt so good. In fact, he didn't remember *ever* feeling so good. What had happened to him?

Then, Dad realized that he also felt light. Really light. So light, that he felt like he was floating.

Oh! He *was* floating! Or flying, he couldn't really tell. *Which was it? And how? What was happening here?*

He was somehow floating upward. He was rising above his bed and, soon, he could see his sick, skinny, body lying curled up in the twin bed in his room. It looked pathetic. He suddenly felt so sorry for that sick person lying on that bed, looking so terrible.

Just then, he felt someone else's presence. A man, who felt familiar to him, but who Dad couldn't recognize, stood right next to him. The man had no facial features, but he spoke to Dad in the Native language, in Ojibwe. He addressed Dad by name—*Da Di Gay Guu Neb*—and told him he would be his guide. He was there to help him through this. The man's lips did not move, but Dad *knew* what the man was saying. He also knew, somehow, that everything was going to be alright.

They were joined by another faceless man and Dad knew that the second man was there to help him too, even though no words were spoken. He could still hear them, somehow.

The men stood, floated really, on either side of him. And then very quickly, all three of them flew through the roof of his room. He looked down and could see the whole building.

Dad knew they were going higher and higher in the air based on the size of what he saw down below. The houses, the cars, all the rest of the Tribal buildings, the lake and then Spirit Island...everything was getting smaller.

It reminded him of looking out an airplane window when you take off. Except this time, there was no plane. There were just three men rising upwards and moving forward at a very fast pace.

The whole Village looked so tiny.

Warrior Spirit Rising

Dad felt like the men were showing him around, and they indicated that he was supposed to go through a doorway off in the distance. But he wanted to be shown more. He didn't really want to leave. Again, without words, but with complete understanding, they turned away from the door. They led Dad back down towards the Village and to a building. There were so many cars outside the building. Dad wanted to see what was going on.

They didn't go through the doors. Instead, they entered through the walls and Dad felt only the great, light, happy feeling he had felt since waking up. Once inside, the setting looked familiar. They were at a wake. The kind held when someone passes on—or dies, as most non-Natives would say.

There were many people around and Dad was curious to know whose wake it was. He looked closer at the coffin...and saw himself.

He wasn't sure what to think, and he didn't have time to process what he saw. Immediately, and with lightning speed, they were no longer at the wake, but looking down on the gravesite in the Nett Lake Cemetery.

Everything happened so fast, all in the blink of an eye. It was as if there was no space and no time.

Dad was looking down on the people who had gathered there at the gravesite. There were so many people there, but he could see his kids, and even his ex-wife, crying over his grave. (Years later, while telling me this story again, he almost actually grinned as he said, "Even your mom was crying at my grave.")

He wanted to reach down and tell his family that everything was okay. He was feeling so much better, now. His aches and pains were gone. His spirit was free.

In that moment, Dad felt somehow happy, even though he was confused about what was actually happening. Was he dead? He didn't feel dead. He felt more alive than he had ever felt in his life. He felt joy. He felt happy. He felt love, in fact, he was full of love. He wanted to share this feeling with everyone.

Dianna Good Sky

His two guides were at his side again, and Dad knew it was time to leave. They turned toward the doorway they had pointed out before and the last thing he felt them say was to not look back. "Go now, and don't look back, you'll hear everyone crying and if you look back, you'll get stuck."

As soon as he opened the door, Dad suddenly felt even lighter than before. He felt like he was flying really fast, and he could see the bright white light that was at the other side of what seemed like a tunnel.

He kept his focus on that light.

His happiness became amplified. He felt so light! He felt so good! There was no pain, there was only peace. He was filled with an overwhelming sense of calm and gratitude. And love.

Not quite sure of how or what was happening, he was still very happy.

He began to see people as he passed by them. They had sticks in their mouths. They didn't look very happy and he could feel a difference between how he felt and what they looked like. He was glad when he stopped seeing them, even though he wished he could help them. He instinctively knew that they had gotten stuck. They were lost.

Eventually he came to a bridge and crossed over. He saw many more people, all miserable, and he knew they were unhappy. As he continued on, he realized that these people were all him. Each individual represented him at various times of his life when he'd either had bad experiences or had done something bad to others.

He recognized himself in their faces and was saddened by what he saw. It was like he was given a view of himself that he couldn't see before. He did not like what he saw. Their faces reflected anger. Sadness. Hopelessness. Regret. Shame. Fear. Grief. Despair. Jealousy. Just as he was beginning to comprehend the enormity of what he saw, they disappeared.

All of a sudden, the tunnel stopped.

Dad stood facing a fast-moving river, and there, on the far bank, was a huge white dog. The dog ignored him. Dad wasn't sure what to do, except wait.

He began to wonder why the majestic dog, which appeared to be as big as a pony, was ignoring him. In that moment of contemplation, he realized that it was because he had done wrong in his time on earth. He had hurt people and animals.

Dad paused in that knowledge, the knowledge that comes when you realize you have done things you shouldn't have done. He had done some pretty bad things—especially while he was drunk—especially to his kids.

He wasn't quite sure what to do next. He did feel very bad for what he had done, yet, at the same time, he also knew that everything would be fine. It was an interesting feeling, that simultaneous knowledge of remorse and redemption.

As soon as Dad experienced that feeling of remorse and regret, and the pain he had caused others, especially those that he loved, the dog stood up and started to cross the river. Dad knew the dog was coming to pick him up.

The dog didn't say anything, Dad just knew. He was starting to get used to communicating with his thoughts.

Once the beautiful, pure white, dog reached him, Dad climbed on his back and they started back across the river. As they were crossing, Dad turned and saw big boulders rolling violently in the water. He could see just how bad the current was, and he was incredibly grateful to be on the dog instead of trying to get across by himself.

They were about halfway across the river when Dad noticed the serpent bridge. He knew that was where the *Midewiwin* people went—the medicine men. He was not a *Mide*. He knew he couldn't go there.

Once the dog got him across the river, he let him off and Dad was faced with a fork in the road. Somehow, he knew he had to take the road on the right. So, he did. It was quite a wonderful feeling to simply "know" everything, and he rather enjoyed it.

Dianna Good Sky

Dad felt as if he was floating again and traveling very fast. Again, he could see the brightness in the distance ahead.

Dad realized that there were people on each side of him again, as he floated down the road. He started recognizing them as those who had passed on already: his aunts, uncles, cousins. They were all nodding at him as he passed. Then he noticed his dad, and both sets of grandparents. He knew that they were acknowledging him; in his mind, he could hear them calling him by his nickname. *Way Jape.* He heard this many times as he floated by.

Soon he came to Grandpa Burnside, the one who gave him the charcoal and the one who named him. No words were spoken, and his grandfather lacked any facial features, but Dad recognized him and heard his voice in his head, "Grandchild, you have arrived, but you must go further."

It is hard to describe a soul and the communication that can take place between souls, between spirits. Grandpa Burnside had no facial features, no voice, but he still communicated with Dad, guiding him forward. Grandpa Burnside, whether through thought or feeling, indicated toward another bright, white light in the distance. Dad knew that was where he needed to go.

Dad went on, and eventually, he came to a huge wigwam, which was glowing with almost fluorescent light. There was a man in the middle of the wigwam. He had long white hair and his hair touched the floor. At first, Dad thought the man was dressed all in white. Then he realized that the man was glowing, he was the source of the luminescent light.

Dad knelt down in front of him with a sudden knowledge that this was the Creator. Dad was delighted to see him.

"Ni Gi iPii Dagoshin," Dad said. "I have arrived."

"Gaawiin Noozhis. Azhegiiwen." The man replied. He, too, was faceless and glowing as bright as the wigwam around him. "No grandchild. You must return from where you came."

Dad continued: *"Nindibi iidog. Nigwiinawi-inendam."* He felt stunned. "I don't know where I am! I don't know what to think."

This figure, whose white hair fell to the floor, said:

"Geyaabi. Gii Zhii Du Whin. Wii Doo Ko Daadiwin Gi JI Anishiinabeg." "Go back, child, it's not your time. You're not finished yet. You have to help the people."

Dad didn't want to let go of this newfound peace that he was feeling, but he knew he had to listen to the man with the white hair.

Even though he couldn't quite understand what was happening, he turned to start back to where he came from as the old man motioned for him to go. He felt equally unsure, yet confident that he could figure out how to get back.

As he passed by his relatives once more, they waved to him and called without speaking. "Go finish, there's a lot of work you have to do."

He nodded to them along the way.

At the river, the dog didn't hesitate to let Dad climb on his back as he carried him across the rough water. Dad didn't see anyone on the way home. He realized he was on a different path than the one he traveled before.

Then he woke up.

Came to.

Was born again.

I don't know, but he was forever changed.

Once back in his physical, earthly body, he once again felt terrible. He was weak. He felt sick, and he couldn't believe that it was mere moments (or was it? He had no idea how long he had been gone) before that he had felt only love and pure joy. While his physical body didn't seem to be healed at all, he knew something had changed: He had a job to do. He wasn't exactly sure what that job was, but he knew he had one, and he knew he needed to be sober to do it.

It took everything in him to lift himself up from his bed. He was so weak. Slowly, he made his way to the door. He looked back at the dirty, disgusting rooms of his apartment and knew it was the last time it would ever be like that.

Dianna Good Sky

Dad gradually made his way out of the main entrance of the Elderly Unit, clutching the walls to keep himself steady. Once he opened the door, he noticed a huge staff leaning against the exterior wall. He had never noticed it there before. He was grateful for the walking assistance as he reached for the staff and used it as leverage as he crossed the road to find Axel.

Axel was the Chemical Dependency counselor who happened to live across the road from Dad. Despite the short distance between their homes, Dad wasn't sure he could make it. He slowly crossed the street and managed to make it up one step, and then another until he stood in front of Axel's house. He used his walking staff to knock on the door.

Axel didn't come right away, so Dad knocked on the door again, balancing precariously on the steps. Finally, Axel opened the door to find Gene Goodsky in front of him, barely able to stand.

"I am looking at death," Axel said. "Come on in Gene, come on in."

Axel helped Dad walk up the remaining flight of stairs and into the house. It didn't take long for Axel to understand why Gene was there. He was ready to stop drinking, but he knew he needed help. Dad wanted Axel to take him to MashKaWisen, the residential treatment facility where Native Americans go to get sober. This wasn't the first time Axel had walked this journey with my dad, but he somehow knew this time was different. He looked Dad in the eye and said, "I believe you are ready this time. Let me make the arrangements and I'll drive you down there."

Dad rested while Axel went about making phone calls. As he sat there, however, Dad suddenly realized that he might need some money.

Shit.

He didn't have any. At all. But he knew where he might get some.

Mom worked at the Community Center in the Village, which wasn't far from Axel's place. Dad explained to Axel that he needed to go see Arlene. After that, he would be waiting at his home for Axel to come take him to MashKaWisen.

He was already feeling a bit stronger—thanks to some toast and coffee from Axel—so he grabbed his walking stick and slowly made his way to the building where my mom was at work.

When she saw Dad approach her desk, she gave him a look of disgust, but let him sit down anyway. He told her that he was going in for treatment, and that this was going to be the last time. He saw her soften slightly, and he could see in her eyes that she believed him. He did seem different this time, she said. So, she wrote a check for $50, made out to him.

He was right.

It would be the last time.

That was the day his hair started turning stark white.

Dianna Good Sky

15
A RETURN TO HOME

When Dad checked himself into MishKaWasen, he knew his life would never be the same. His experience the night before left him markedly changed—even if still unsure about what was happening to him. One thing was certain: he needed to get sober.

He knew he couldn't do the work he was called to do if he was drunk. Although, he had no idea what exactly he was called to do. He took the only logical first step and went to treatment.

His first task was cleaning up his life. Dad felt strongly that this was something he had to do alone—without any outside influence or input. He asked the treatment center to hold all his mail, not take any phone calls, and no one whatsoever would be allowed to visit. He wouldn't even take any mail that I sent him from boot camp. Not that I ever knew this.

Mail can be a very big deal, especially in a season of transition and isolation. I was learning this while at boot camp. I received so many letters during that time that I became the envy of my fellow Navy enlistees. Mom, who was familiar with military life, had organized to have my relatives send me mail frequently. Meanwhile, Dad was requesting no one bother him, even with a simple letter. To be honest, had we known what he was going through at the time, we likely would have thought it was just another trip to treatment, same as before. But something was clearly different.

During the treatment, Dad had many major breakthroughs. He relived difficult memories of hunger, isolation, alcohol abuse, and his dad's remains strewn across the train tracks. He had to navigate memories of Vietnam and learn to manage the ongoing PTSD. It could not have been easy. But freedom is always hard-won. By the end, Dad knew alcohol no longer had a grip on him—he simply knew it.

The day he checked out of the treatment center, the director, Art Holmes, spent four hours with Dad. The usual checkout process takes one hour, at most. Art pushed Dad to release any last bit of crap that he was still holding onto. They talked, Art asked the tough questions, and Dad processed everything. And then Art simply let him cry it out. Dad is still very grateful that Art allowed him that time to unravel all that was inside of him, and finally let it go.

After leaving the safety net of the treatment center, however, Dad knew he wasn't strong enough to return to Nett Lake and all his drinking buddies. He decided to move to the little town of Tower. Tower sits near the Vermillion sector of the Bois Forte Reservation—the tribe's lands make up three distinct sectors, with Nett Lake being the largest and most populated— and Dad had a sober cousin who lived there: Isabel, and her husband, Ken Strong.

They welcomed him with open arms. Dad looked forward to being around friendly, sober members of the family. And he was happy to take up carpentry again—Ken and Isabel were in the process of building a new home.

Dad started attending AA meetings every week in order to build up his resistance to alcohol, but the truth is, he found it wasn't difficult to keep away from alcohol because he was working on his purpose. He still had no idea what the old man meant when he said, "Go back, child...you have to help the people." But somehow, that didn't matter. What mattered was that he sought the answers, wherever they may be.

At the treatment center, one of the most valuable tools they give the Natives is a reminder of who they are. They reflect on the Pow Wow circle, tradition, ceremony, things that Dad used to have in his life, but society and alcohol took away from him.

If he was meant to help the people, then Dad determined that he would need to return to his culture, to an understanding of the Anishinabeg. He kept working with the Strongs, attending AA meetings, and he began visiting the Elders—something he hadn't done since he was a young boy.

Eventually, Dad knew that he needed to be in Nett Lake. Where else could it be that he "had a job to do" where he could "help the people"? He settled back in the Village and began living with an unswerving commitment to help others. Almost immediately after returning home, he began holding AA meetings in Nett Lake. It was definitely a time of transition, not only for Dad, but also for the people of Nett Lake. They were used to seeing him walking around the Village drunk, disheveled, stinking. Or trying to hawk his things on the street just to get money for booze. Or bumming a ride into Orr to go to the liquor store. It did not take long for them to realize that he was actually sober, and with each passing week, as he held the meetings, they realized that he very well could stay that way.

By the time I returned home on leave in September, Dad had been sober for six months. He had returned to the "Wrinkle Ranch" in Nett Lake and began working as a Conservation Officer for the Forestry Division of the Tribe. He told me that he was able to get that job because of two very important people: Dan Morrison and Gary Donald.

In 1980, Gary Donald was the Tribal Chairman, Dan Morrison was the Tribal Secretary/Treasurer for the Reservation Business Council—now called the Reservation Tribal Council—the governing body for the Bois Forte Band of Chippewa. Gary had a healthy respect for the traditional ways and for the Goodsky family. He didn't like what he had seen happen to Dad; he had watched far too many lives ruined by alcohol.

Dad knew that since he was returning to Nett Lake, he would not only need a job, but he would need one that was in service to others. He applied for the position of Conservation Officer. When they received his application, both Gary and Dan gave him an ultimatum: they would be happy to give him a chance, but that was it. He'd get one chance. If he screwed it up, they'd never back him again.

Dad left their offices not only breathing a sigh of relief, but also with a deep sense of gratitude to be given a chance.

It was during that trip home, prior to my deployment to Brawdy, Wales, that I first heard Dad's story. His crazy-ass story. I really thought he was high.

I was visiting him at his home, and I'll never forget the look on his face as he began sharing his experience with me. It was almost as if he wasn't sure he wanted to tell me but felt that he must. I'm sure my baffled expression didn't help matters. Despite my surprise, afterward, I wrote down everything he told me, and filed it away.

After our conversation, and Dad's declaration that he would never drink again, he suggested that we all get together and go to dinner before I left the country. So, we did.

We all crammed into Mom's car, the entire family. We hadn't all been together like that, in such close proximity, for years. Mom and Dad sat in the front with my son, Francis, in between them. Lela, Curtis, and I squashed into the back seat. This was going to be a long drive.

In reality, it felt so good to be sitting with my siblings and laughing and carrying on, just like old times—a long time ago. But

Dianna Good Sky

then something unexpected happened. Dad decided to perform a ceremony.

It was the first time that I saw my dad perform a ceremony—a real, Native ceremony. What he tried to teach us growing up, in his drunken state, had nothing to do with ceremony, or anything traditional for that matter.

Before we started the drive, Dad pulled out some tobacco and began speaking in Anishinaabemowin. It immediately reminded me of his drunk self, yelling at us to "Dance! Move your feet!" I still had many bad memories, and a deep seeded aversion to knowing anything about our culture. I really didn't want anything to do with this Indian stuff.

I asked what the heck he was doing, and Lela told me that he was making an offering. My sister and brother watched in appreciation while I stared at them, and then quieted my thoughts. Maybe this was different than before. It seemed different. Sort of.

When I asked Dad about the ceremony, he said, "That was a prayer for safe travels. I made an offering to the Spirits who watch over us. For all of us. And also, for when you go overseas."

I leaned back in my seat and wondered if this kind of prayer worked. And also, what did tobacco have to do with it? He had never used tobacco when we were growing up. I had many questions and I kind of thought his level of crazy had escalated. I couldn't seem to shake the sense of dread from our midnight cultural lessons.

We arrived at the restaurant—*The Elroy*—so my questions were put aside, along with the storm of emotions I felt—I shoved them all down, deep inside. I could deal with those later. It was clear, despite what I was feeling, that Dad was somehow different. As it turned out, that was just the beginning.

I left for my duty station in Wales not long after our family dinner. Communication was limited back then, especially if you lived overseas, but Mom kept me posted on how Dad was doing.

I think she wavered between shock and hope for a very long time. I mean, while there was no love lost between them, he was our Dad. She wanted him to be a good dad. Don't all mothers?

She sent word that he started work as the cultural teacher at the Nett Lake School. I was surprised that he could be a teacher. I had seen his return to his cultural roots since he became sober, but I knew he didn't have a college degree. A teacher? And, in both the elementary and the high school?

After a while, Mom also told me that Dad had a pretty serious girlfriend, Rose. He had met her while they both worked at the Nett Lake School. He and Rose eventually married, and together they chose to clear the trees and brush that had overtaken Dad's family home in Sugar Bush. They were going to live there. A return to his roots, for sure.

It also signaled that healing had taken place. So many good and bad memories were created in that beautiful little area surrounded by maple trees, blueberries, and lakeshore. Even though so much had been taken away—the laws and the rules, the boarding schools and the outlawed religion, the alcohol and the devastation—there, in the North Woods of Minnesota, Ojibwe culture didn't just survive. It also came back to life.

Dianna Good Sky

16

THE GIFT OF MEDICINE

Spiritual messages continued to pursue Dad, both recalling and revealing his earlier childhood experiences with Ojibwe traditions. He worked tirelessly to heal, grow, and help others, doing the work the old man had told him to do, or at least, part of it.

Dad also knew that there was more for him to do. Something was missing, some connection to himself or his heritage that he couldn't quite articulate.

The answer came unexpectedly in the form of a spiritual message. It was anything but coincidence.

It was a Friday afternoon when Dad's friend Harold Lightfeather stopped by to see him at the little building where he held the AA meetings. Harold's friends like to call him Kmart, because he was always talking about going to Kmart. But on this day, Kmart asked Dad to go somewhere else entirely.

He was headed to the Dryden Pow Wow in Canada, and invited Dad to go with him. Since he had no other plans, Dad was happy to go. He had never been, and he thought it would be a good experience.

Pow Wows were making a sudden resurgence at the time, a trend that continues into the present day in both Canada and the United States. While Pow Wows as a spiritual or religious practice had been deemed illegal for decades, some tribes either subverted the law entirely, and carried on with traditional practice, or created a sort of modified Pow Wow that focused on dancing and connection rather than tradition.

In 1978, the American Indian Religious Freedom Act removed the legal binding that had hindered spiritual practices for generations. Unfortunately, so many of those practices had already been lost or buried. By 1980, some Pow Wows were merely a fun gathering, a competition, or a way to monetize what remained of the culture.

Other Pow Wows began to represent a return to traditions. There were those who still knew the old ways, who understood the importance of bringing back the culture. Just like Grandpa Burnside. Just like Dad was starting to discover.

Kmart and Dad packed the car with camping supplies and headed north to Ontario. They set up their campsite once they arrived and decided to head over to the Pow Wow circle where there were already a few drummers getting ready. They settled in on the bleachers to listen to the drum music, as the singers were warming up. They sat there for a while, soaking it up, and soon went to bed with the sound of the drums still pounding in the distance.

The next morning after breakfast, they went back to the grounds and sat close to the Pow Wow arbor, where the dancing would take place. Dad noticed an old man, an elder, sitting near the arbor with a drum in front of him on the ground, smoking a pipe. As the elder finished his pipe he looked up at Dad and Kmart, stood and walked toward them, holding their gaze. They noticed he was holding tobacco in his hand.

Dianna Good Sky

As the old man approached them, he held out his hand with the tobacco inside and spoke to them. It was immediately clear that he only spoke Anishinaabemowin.

"Do you understand? Do you understand Anishinaabemowin?" he asked.

Dad replied, "Yes, I understand."

"Will you come and help me?" the old man asked.

"Yes. We will."

The old man gave Dad and Kmart a pipe full of tobacco, and they followed him to his drum. Once they were settled around the drum, they sat smoking the pipe.

"Geez I wonder what I should sing?" the old man said in Anishinaabemowin. "Maybe I should sing something fancy like a square-dancing song so the girls will show their bloomers."

Dad's eyes got really big as he thought, "Wow! A medicine man talking like that?"

Then the old man started laughing. He had seen Dad's expression.

"It's good." He said, "The spirits would like to see you laughing, they like to hear crazy sayings because they laugh, too."

Dad relaxed as he thought about that.

The old man asked them if they knew any songs, and while Dad's experience with native singing was buried in long ago memories, he said he'd be able to follow along.

So, the old man started pounding the drum, and Dad began to recall the music. He found it very interesting that he could remember them. They were old, old, Anishinabe songs.

After a little while, the old man turned to Dad, and with a very serious look of delight on his face, he said, "I've been waiting for you."

Dad just sat there, staring at the old man. "I've been waiting for you," he said again. "I have to give you something. Come over to my house."

Dad had never seen the old man in his life. What could he possibly mean? But he accepted the invitation. The man was an elder, after all, and Dad knew that he should go simply out of respect. He knew the old man's invitation was more of a command, even if nicely put. He wouldn't have dreamt of declining the invitation.

The old man had said, "I have something for you." Dad immediately recognized that the man meant to give him a gift. Even though he still wasn't familiar with all of the old ways, he had gotten fairly used to things just happening to him—these spiritual messages—and he knew to just allow these things to happen.

Once they got to the house, Dad and Kmart sat on the bench outside while the old man went inside. When he came out, he was carrying a plant.

He asked Dad if he knew what the plant was called.

Yes. He did.

Then he told Dad that the plant was used for heart medicine and he would teach Dad what to do with it. The plant was made to help those who experienced heart attacks and strokes. Dad was excited and honored.

"I've been waiting a long time for you," the old man said.

Dad knew it was a great honor to receive this gift and he looked forward to learning about the healing properties of the plant. He was reminded of his childhood passion for learning about living things, especially the local plant life.

Yet, he had no idea how this man could have been waiting for him, or how he even knew who he was. But he trusted him. He knew he was supposed to be there, right there with that old man at that exact moment. He just knew.

Dad went back to his car and collected a few items for *Bi Gi Ji Gun*, an offering. He was glad he always carried items that could be used as an offering for the unexpected receipt of gifts. He dug around and found his tobacco, wild rice, a pocketknife, a twenty-dollar bill, and a makeshift "dish" with cookies and berries that he and Kmart snacked on during the drive up north.

He returned to the house to present his *Bi Gi Ji Gun* to the old man.

Dianna Good Sky

"The tobacco I'm offering you is for what you gave me, the medicine, the heart medicine," Dad explained.

The old man took it from him and said *"Howah! Nee E Wah!"*

"Good! That's it! That's the way to do it!"

The old man took Dad's tobacco and loaded up his pipe. He smoked the tobacco and then sang a song, and both Dad and Kmart helped him sing. It was a healing song.

"There, that plant came," the man said, when the song was finished. "The spirit of the plant came. He accepted your tobacco and your food and your offerings. Now this is yours." He indicated the plant. "You can have this. You can help people that have a heart attack and strokes."

Dad was humbled. This was a significant moment, and he knew it.

Later, he would try to explain to me the difference between spiritual messages and coincidence.

"To anyone else, it's a coincidence, but to the people that understand the spirituality... Someone told my friend to say to me, 'Let's go check out the Pow Wow.' Somebody came and told him, and right away I accepted. I said, 'Okay.' That's not coincidence. Those are Spiritual messages."

He was right. The heart medicine gift would turn out to help many of his people and even those outside his Native circle. Nothing about Dad's life is a coincidence.

17
TEACHER
1981

In 1981, there was a job opening for a Cultural teacher in both Nett Lake and in the high school in Orr. It was a new program that the Reservation was implementing. They received funding to help Tribes regain the culture that had been ripped away by the boarding schools and the laws. An attempt at restitution, I suppose.

The goal of the program was to teach the Ojibwe language, culture, and traditions in the schools, and hopefully infuse cultural revitalization on the Rez. Due to the nature of the program, having a college degree was not part of the requirement for the applicants. What was listed, rather, was Ojibwe language fluency.

The teaching position excited Dad. He felt deep down inside that *this* was part of the path he was supposed to take. He was fluent in Ojibwe, and he grew up in the old ways. Surely this would qualify him. He called the school and found out that there were already sixteen applicants. He thought there was no way they'd pick him, mainly due to his recent history and reputation as a drunk. While he thought he didn't have a chance in hell, he applied anyway.

He was still unsure if they would hire him and decided to get some input from Dan and Gary, who had taken a chance on him when he first became sober. He remembered making a promise to himself that he would never let them down and decided to give them a call.

Dad trusted Dan and Gary—and at that point, considered them his friends. He also respected them as leaders in the Tribe and knew they would give him honest feedback. He wanted to know; did they think the teaching position would be a good fit for him?

He was about to embark on a whole new career, something he'd never done before. Dad was a carpenter, by trade, not a teacher. Yet, he knew this was his next step. As long as it was the right fit. Dan and Gary were both glad to hear Dad had applied for the job and thought he would be a very good Cultural Teacher. They had watched Dad progress in his sobriety and were very hopeful for his future. Their words of encouragement gave Dad confidence. There was a solid level of trust starting to develop between these leaders. They knew he was straightening out and they looked forward to what he could do for the community.

The next morning, right at eight o'clock, the phone rang. It was the Nett Lake Elementary principal. "Do you want to come in for an interview?" he asked.

"Interview for what?" Dad said.

"The culture teacher, that teaching job."

Dad wasn't sure what to say. He had an interview that morning and that afternoon the school board met to discuss the applicants. Afterward, they called Dad to tell him the good news. "Out of sixteen applicants, you were the most qualified because of your fluent speaking. You lived the life instead of going to college. We would like to hire you."

He was so excited that when they asked him how soon he could start, he said, "Right now!"

There wasn't a curriculum built for this program, so Dad and his new assistant, Shirley, went to work building one. When Dad asked the principal what his expectations were, or if he needed to work within a set program, the principal simply pointed at Dad and said, "You're the teacher. I'm only the white guy." And that was that.

Every week, Dad and Shirley worked together to build worksheets and language flash cards for the class. Dad began to see how deeply Anishinabe ways had been buried, and the distinct loss of the language, so they tried to cover a wide range of categories, everything from all living beings, plants, animals, birds, and fish to ricing, beading, and maple sugar tapping.

I was proud of him when Mom told me he would be teaching. And honestly, I really hoped he wouldn't relapse. Even though I had believed him when he said he was never going to drink again—I saw the truth of it in his eyes—history provided a different story. I am not sure how many years passed before I realized that, in fact, he wasn't going to drink again. I just hoped that he wouldn't hurt anyone, if he did fall off the wagon.

Besides teaching the younger kids at Nett Lake Elementary, part of his role was to teach the older students at Orr High School in the afternoon. One popular teacher at Orr was Nancy Parvi, and she and Dad became fast friends. Dad also developed an immediate friendship with Mickey Elverum, a teacher who had just started working there when I was in the ninth grade.

When Dad talks about those days, how the three of them would walk down the halls together, with Nancy in the middle, his mind seems to go to a faraway place. He recalls their friendships with such love and gratitude, you can feel it in the room when he speaks. They would walk around the school together during the lunch hour, laughing, talking, "raising Cain" as my dad likes to put it. But they were also doing so much more than that. Together, one Native, a white man, and a white woman, they were slowly eradicating racism from the school. At a time and in a place where

Dianna Good Sky

racism and prejudice were rampant, and had been since the opening of the school, this was a very unique situation.

As they roamed the halls together, Dad, Nancy, and Mickey would break up the little cliques that were all over the school. These cliques looked just like they have always looked at Orr High School: groups of Whites and groups of Indians. Each wary of the other, guarded. The harsh reality of a mixed school where one group knew nothing of the other. Except what they were most likely taught by their parents to stick to their own kind. Dad and the others would tell the kids, "Hey, break that up!" And if you've ever heard Dad use his "stern" voice, there is no doubt that those kids jumped and broke up their cliques.

Dad and the others didn't realize that the example they were setting—three friends who didn't see each other's "color"—would eventually bridge the race gap between not only Orr and Nett Lake, but also Nett Lake and the other neighboring communities. It started in Orr High School, in the hallways, with three friends walking and laughing together.

It wasn't long before the non-Native students at Orr started hanging around Dad's class, wanting to join in. They knew they were welcome there, and they liked hearing what he had to say. At first, the students would stop at the door to listen. Then they'd ask if they could come in. After a while, they'd just stop in and sit right down, either to bead or to listen to Dad's stories. Soon, Dad became a mentor to anyone who needed a listening ear, some advice, a place to relax, or sometimes a place to hide. His classroom and his presence were a source of strength to many.

After about two years of teaching at the high school, the difference in the relationships between the Natives and non-Natives was remarkable. But years of racism and its solid grip on young minds—and old ones—would not go away so easily. Tensions still existed, but everyone could see that things were changing.

While teaching at the Nett Lake school, Dad met his future wife, Rose. It all started when she asked him to make medicine for a family member. Dad was building a reputation as a healer as he continued to learn how to make the traditional medicines.

When he delivered his second batch of a special medicinal tea, Rose started asking questions. They developed a friendship that eventually led to marriage. I was happy for him, even though I was stationed far away and couldn't attend the wedding. I was thrilled, actually. Not only had he found love, but his journey in sobriety was holding up and he was doing so much good for so many people.

Eventually, Dad told me that he and Rose were going to build a home in Sugar Bush. It had been over thirty years since anyone had lived there. Removing the overgrowth, alone, was going to be a tremendous undertaking. Not to mention the lack of electricity or running water. He and Rose worked tirelessly clearing the trees and brush and moving the heavy cambrian rocks to make a road. They even cleared the area where Dad and his family used to fish, right on the water's edge. Only occasionally did Dad relive some of his more troubling memories. Like the night his sisters and their boyfriends made fun of him for stumbling while drinking. That fishing spot was the same spot where he passed out, promising himself that he would never drink again.

As Dad saw what was happening at the high school in Orr—the racial tensions slowly dying and the students' eagerness to learn and participate in the culture—he knew that more could be done. He saw an opportunity to bridge the cultural gap even further. He asked Nancy if he could invite the Orr kids to some of the camps he was doing in Sugar Bush. Nancy readily agreed.

Once Sugar Bush was cleared enough for use, Dad began hosting camps for his students. He would teach them about the wild rice, and demonstrate the process of harvesting, parching, jigging, and fanning. The tradition of ricing was slowly fading, so Dad would have the students join in the process so that they could appreciate the work that goes into this culturally significant food.

Dianna Good Sky

In the spring, he would teach them about sugar maple tapping and the traditional ways the Anishinabeg made maple sugar and maple syrup. Like the wild rice, he taught them the process from start to finish, with auntie Alma, who had later built a house in Sugar Bush, helping out whenever the kids were there.

What started as small camps and field trips to Sugar Bush eventually grew into so much more. Dad took the students on trips to learn about the plants, then to mini Pow Wows that he would coordinate, sometimes even on canoe trips. He took every opportunity he could to get the kids together, the Natives and the non-Natives. He decided that the only way for the kids to see past the color of their skin was to show them that we are all the same, we are just people.

During the camps and the field trips, he would encourage the students to intermingle by pairing them together: Native with a non-Native, boys with girls. For Dad, not only was it important for them to get to know each other from a cultural standpoint, but also from the standpoint of girls and boys being equal. He wanted the boys to know that the girls were just as capable, and the girls to know that the boys could be gentlemen. It sounds a bit odd, but Dad, even in his forward thinking, was very traditional.

Before long, non-Natives began dating Natives, something fairly unusual for such a racially charged town. Our prejudices were as old as the surrounding maples.

Somehow, these cultural lessons—the field trips and the classes, the camps and the shared experiences—had a radical impact on the community. In a school that used to be rife with blatant racism, the sharp edges of a racist culture began to dull. In time, it would be a thing of the past. At least while Dad was there.

After he had been teaching for a while, Dad was approached with the idea of getting his teaching certificate. He contacted the Minnesota Board of Educators to find out what he had to do in order for this to happen. The certification would mean Dad could be paid as a teacher, not just a culture teacher under a grant. It would also mean that he could start building his retirement.

Dad called me when his certificate was awarded. He was the first person in the state of Minnesota to be awarded a teaching certificate without a college degree.

We both knew why.

He lived his life in the old ways. There were no schools whose curriculum could match that.

With his certificate in hand, and his reputation as a teacher growing, Dad was soon asked to teach Ojibwe culture in the local colleges. His schedule was already so full that his only free time was at night and on weekends. But he was eager to teach and before long, he was teaching at three local colleges. Now, I say local, but this is the North Woods of Minnesota we're talking about. The colleges were at least seventy miles away. His schedule was jammed packed.

Dad taught at Nett Lake Elementary every morning. Then, he would drive to Orr to teach the High school classes in the afternoon. In the evenings, he would drive to whichever college he had for the semester (sometimes two at once) and teach Ojibwe. He often wouldn't get home until well past midnight. He would be up at 5:00 a.m. the next day to do it all over again.

His purpose—the work he had come back to do—became more and more clear as he sought to revitalize his own cultural understanding, and then pass that along to others. He was a new man, or maybe he had simply become the man he was always meant to be. The original man. Anishinabe.

Dianna Good Sky

18

HEALER

After receiving the gift of heart medicine at the Pow Wow in Canada, Dad endeavored to learn more about the old ways—the traditional medicinal practices of the Anishinabeg. His reputation began to spread around the Village, and outside of the Bois Forte community that he could help with traditional medicine.

Dad began building relationships with the elders, and in particular, a medicine man named Jimmy Jackson. It was through Jimmy that Dad received another gift of medicine.

Rose experienced a particularly harsh migraine one evening. She was sitting up in bed, crying, and Dad asked, "What's the matter?"

When she said her head was really painful, he asked, "Is that the migraine headache?"

"Yeah."

"Well, let's get dressed," he said, "and we'll go see Jimmy Jackson."

It was four o'clock in the morning. Dad made breakfast while Rose gathered two five-pound bags of rice to take with them. It was ricing season and together they had collected more than enough to get them through the year. They always carried extra *Bi Gii Ji Gun*, some gifts for offerings, as well as tobacco, just in case they needed to make a ceremonial dish. The rice would be part of their *Bi Gii Ji Gun*.

Jimmy lived in Brookston, just east of Cloquet, MN, nearly one hundred miles south of Sugar Bush. When Dad and Rose arrived, Jimmy greeted them and accepted their offerings, laying them down carefully to rest until the ceremony.

Dad and Rose followed Jimmy into a dark room, and he asked Rose to lie down on the bed. The lights were off, and the room was completely dark—so dark they couldn't even see one another.

What Dad could see, however, was Jimmy's small medicine drum, about six inches in diameter. Jimmy picked it up and started rattling the little drum and singing.

At the same moment he started singing, a little light appeared in the room. The light was the size of a quarter. It began moving up and down, as though it were dancing to the rattle of the drum. It moved and shifted and then went around Rose's head. Dad watched as the light circled her head four times.

"I saw that, and my eyes must have been just wide open." Dad told me, years later. "I was just so amazed that that little light was there and appearing as if it were dancing. It went around four times and then, zoom! It went out."

After Jimmy finished singing, he said, *Sun Ah Gut An E Pay E In.* "It's strong, what's going on inside of your head. Very, very severe headaches," He said. "I can fix that."

He turned to Dad and asked, "Do you know what *Bii Sun Da Goos* (tamarack) is?"

"Yeah," Dad replied.

"Do you know what a *Mush Kii Gwa Tig* (white pine) is?"

"Yeah."

"And you know cedar?"

Dad nodded. "Yeah."

Then Jimmy began to explain the process to make a migraine medicine. The white pine must be four feet tall and have four branches out on the top. You must pick it and dry it out—all of the different plants must be dry.

"And it also requires Juniper," he said. "They call that *Gaa ga gii wahn dug.*" Dad knew that plant, too.

So, all four plants, Jimmy explained, would make a migraine medicine: *Gaa Ga Gii Wahn Dug,* cedar, tamarack, and white pine. "You dry these up real good," he said. "Put them in the oven. Just the pilot light will be enough heat to dry them up overnight. Then put them in a blender, all the needles in a blender. When you handle that Juniper," he advised, "that *Gaa Ga Gii Wahn Dug,* wear leather gloves because otherwise that will penetrate your fingers."

Once the plants are dried and ground into a powder, they must be warmed and diffused. First, Dad would need to find a round rock, particularly gray rock or granite. He would then need to heat that on top of the stove. To test if the stone was ready, he could drop some water on the stone. If it sizzled, it was ready. The hot stone would go into a cast iron pan, with the ground plants placed on top of the stone. Rose would need to lean over the pan and cover her head with a towel. She should inhale the plants, both through the nose and the mouth, for nearly half an hour.

"It's going to sting your nose and you'll feel it in your mouth," Jimmy said. "That's when it's starting to work."

Jimmy gave Dad enough medicine for two days. He told Dad to use it as a guide so he could make up his own medicine.

"Now you can make this up," he said. "I'm giving this to you so you can help people with the same sickness your wife has."

Before they left Jimmy's, another ceremony had to take place. They made up a spiritual dish and offered the dish, the gifts, and tobacco, as was tradition. The two men spoke in Ojibwe and Dad said, *gah ki gah oh ma eh in.* "For what you taught me, I'm offering you tobacco."

Warrior Spirit Rising

Jimmy put out his hand to receive the tobacco. "OH! *MiiGwetch*, thank you." he said. "That's the way, that's the right thing to do."

Dad gave him the rest of the package of tobacco and Jimmy filled up his pipe. He presented Jimmy with a small dish of food, the 10 pounds of rice, twenty dollars, and a blanket. Jimmy performed the ceremony.

When he finished, he said, "There, they came to accept your tobacco. The spirit of that juniper, the spirit of the cedar, the spirit of the white pine, the spirit of the tamarack, they come to accept your offering. Now it's yours. You can have it. You can use it to help people."

That was Dad's second gift of medicine.

When they returned home, Dad followed Jimmy's instructions and after the second day, Rose's migraine was gone. Dad insisted that she continue the protocol—a complete four-day cycle of using the medicine—and so she did. After that, Rose's migraines were gone completely.

Dad began helping others who were suffering from migraines, eager to share his knowledge and help those in need.

As word spread, people began asking Dad for help. He would deliver medicine to anyone who asked. It didn't seem to matter where he was when they called, if someone needed help, he'd get it to them. Rose used to travel with him on his medicine trips, assisting along the way. They were a good pair, doing exactly what they knew they needed to be doing: helping others.

People wanted to call Dad a medicine man, especially considering all the medicine he was helping them with, but he always denied that. He insists he isn't *Mide*. Instead, he refers to himself as a healer. He explains it this way: a medicine man has two-way communication with the Spirits. He, however, only has one-way communication. He can talk to them, but they don't talk back. Although, he says, when a thought comes to him, as it does, he knows it's from the Spirits. Between you and me? I think he has two-way communications. But hey, he's the boss.

Despite not being *Mide*, Dad sure received a lot of medicinal gifts and training. He continued helping others and learning from Jimmy and many other "old people", both at home and in our homelands of Canada. He developed many relationships across Indian Country that still serve him, and our tribe, well today.

At one time, his mom, Gahmaht, became very ill and was bleeding internally. An x-ray failed to reveal what was happening in her body, so Dad insisted they go to Brookston to see Jimmy Jackson.

It was much like it had been with Rose. Gahmaht laid down on the bed in the dark room, and Jimmy began singing and rattling his drum. Again, the light appeared in the room. It came in like it was dancing, up and down, in perfect time with the rattle of the drum.

This time, the light circled her stomach four times and then disappeared. Jimmy continued to sing. After some time, Jimmy halted his song and turned the lights on in the room.

"They showed me where you are bleeding," he said. "The x-ray could not see it because it's way deep inside of you, where the blood is coming from."

He turned to Dad and began explaining what medicine Gahmaht would need in order to get well. This time, he would need wood chips from the ironwood tree.

Dad collected thirty chips from the ironwood tree and boiled them in spring water, as instructed. In a matter of a couple days, Gahmaht quit bleeding.

That was Dad's third gift of medicine, but it wouldn't be his last.

19
SPIRITUAL ADVISOR

Dad knew that Gahmaht's bleeding issues stemmed from drinking and that only sobriety would help keep her healthy. As he helped her heal using the ironwood medicine, he didn't hesitate to let her know his thoughts. Jimmy had also told her, "When the spirits looked inside of you, and when they came back out, they showed that you got a long time to live if you quit drinking. You can live a long time. You can live to be ninety, anywhere to one hundred years old, but you've got to quit drinking."

Dad tried hard to help his mom and Gahmaht did stay sober for about a year. Dad really enjoyed their time together when she was sober. So did his kids at the elementary school. Grandma Gahmaht helped in the classroom by teaching the kids to bead, how to make birch bark baskets and many other traditional teachings. Of course, she also helped with the conversational Ojibwe language while there. When she started drinking again, the bleeding came back within a few days. She came home after four days away, hungover.

"Are you bleeding?" he asked. She said yes, and so he made her more of the ironwood medicine.

"There, now you got to quit. Try." he told her. "I know it's hard. It's difficult to quit drinking. I know that. But once you make up your mind, that's it. Then you are going to be able to leave it alone."

He reminded her that the best way to quit is to stay away from other people and friends that are drinking.

"You know where they are. You have to stay away from them." He said.

"Yeah I know." Gahmaht said. "A lot of times when I'm alone, I get lonesome. All my friends are the ones that are drinking."

Dad understood this well, better than most. That's why he refused communication and visitors during treatment, and why he stayed in Tower afterward. Until he was strong enough. It is also why he continued to host the AA meetings in Nett Lake.

Many of the drinkers in the Village respected Dad's sobriety. They even sought his counsel. They would show up at Dad's place completely drunk, but they never brought their booze inside with them. They just came to visit Dad. One time, his friend Floyd said, "Gene, how did you quit drinking?" He occasionally contemplated telling others and the people at the AA meetings the real reason he stopped drinking but felt that it was better not to.

"I made up my mind." Dad said. "Made up my mind that I'm sick and tired of being sick and tired. I had a good, honorable life before alcohol."

Floyd beckoned Dad to follow him outside. He picked up his bottle of liquor, about half a quart, and He said, "You see this Gene?" He turned the bottle over and poured it out on the ground. "That's it." he said.

"That's good," Dad said to him.

"I'm going to come and talk to you periodically. Whenever I get confused or the urge comes, I'm going to come over and talk to you." Floyd said.

Warrior Spirit Rising

Then Dad said, "And if you need me, come over and talk anytime, no matter if it's two, three o'clock in the morning. Come on over."

And Floyd did. Sometimes he'd call Dad in the early hours of the morning and he'd say, "Can I come over?"

"Yeah," Dad would say. And they would sit and talk until morning.

They talked about everything. They talked about Vietnam. About crazy stories and crazy happenings. Before long they would be laughing, and Dad would ask, "There, did that feel better?"

"I feel a lot better," Floyd would say.

Floyd called on my Dad a lot during that season, but he never went to treatment. Instead, Dad shared the things he learned during his own time in treatment and encouraged Floyd to implement the same tools.

He is sober to this day. Eventually, Floyd became my stepdad.

When I came home on leave once, around 1987, Dad seemed exhausted. He was up at 5:00 a.m. and wouldn't get home until after midnight most nights. Between traveling and teaching at all the schools, providing medicine to people all over the Iron Range, running AA meetings, and counseling anyone who asked him for help, it was hard. But he loved it. And when I told him I was worried about him, he told me that he was fine and that he was following his dad's advice to take care of himself.

He refused to get an answering machine, much to my chagrin. His phone rang at all hours of the day and night, and since I was transferring to Hawaii, I wanted to be able to leave him messages. I thought everyone else should be leaving him messages, too, but he wouldn't budge.

One thing he did acknowledge, however, was that he wouldn't be able to help any more people than he already was.

Before long, however, Dad was presented with another opportunity to serve his people. Gary Donald, Chairman of the tribe, remembered that in the old days, whenever there was any kind of meeting, an elder would bless the meeting. He asked Dad if he would be willing to conduct the blessings over all of the Tribe's meetings. Dad was honored and happy, as always, to help Gary.

Beyond wanting to revitalize this tradition of blessing, Gary and the Council knew that the Tribe needed to return to tradition and knew that Dad was the one to be the Spiritual Advisor for the Tribe. In his new role, Dad would perform blessings at all of the ceremonies, gatherings, Pow Wows, and meetings. In many ways, he would help represent and introduce tradition back into every level of the Tribe, including the Tribal government.

To accommodate his new role, Dad had to adjust the burdensome schedule he had adopted over the previous six years. He chose to stop teaching at the local colleges, but he refused to give up anything else.

Dad loved his new role as Spiritual Adviser. He took it very seriously. Aside from conducting blessings at the Pow Wows, the meetings, and other Tribal gatherings, he also conducted joint funeral services and weddings with the local Christian church. At first, many people, myself included, found this hard to accept. How could a Native ceremony and a Christian ceremony exist side-by-side? It was a valid question. Our relationship with the church has not always been a good one, particularly as it pertains to their involvement in the boarding schools.

My Grandma Jennie was a devout Christian, thanks to her boarding school upbringing. She even influenced my own childhood understanding of faith. While she made sure I attended any Pow Wows that occurred in Nett Lake, she also made sure I attended church with her regularly. I didn't know what it meant to be an Indian, at the time, but I did know what Christians were like, at least I thought I knew. I also knew that I looked forward to the Pow Wows and I hated going to the church.

Grandma's church made us feel bad for being Indian, and that's about all I remember. I cannot even tell you exactly why or how that happened. As time has faded the memories, so have my feelings about it. Except for Wally Olsen. I will always remember Wally Olsen.

He was a beautiful person and he helped form my first understanding of what a Christian was like—a true Christian. Wally was full of love, understanding, and had zero judgement.

My mom used to love telling the story of how she was carrying me out of the Baptist church one Sunday, and Wally was saying goodbye to everyone as they left the church. After he shook my mom's hand and she went past him, he turned to wave at me. Instead of waving back, I stuck up my tiny, two-year-old middle finger. I guess I had already formed my opinion.

Wally chuckled, as he reminded me of this years later when I asked him to be the preacher to marry me and my first husband, in that same church.

Dad still conducts joint funeral services and has established and maintained a wonderful relationship with the last remaining church on the Reservation. There used to be three churches in this tiny village that's the size of a city block. Now, the Baptist church (which I call Wally's church) is the only one remaining.

At first, I found it odd, and a bit uncomfortable, that Dad had such close ties to the church. As we all began to embrace our culture more and more, it felt like our spiritual practices collided— rather than coincided—with the church. So, I challenged him on it. And he told me this: "We are all one. We are all the same, you know. We're all just people. What they call God, we call the Great Spirit. He," Dad pointed upwards with his lower lip, "gave all of us a different way to worship him and a different name. Just like he gave us our different colors of our skin and all our different languages. But he only did that because he had to, for this earthly experience. We are all the same. You have to believe in this. You have to have faith."

From that point on, I was able to see my Christian friends differently. And my Buddhist friends. And, really, my whole world opened up.

Dianna Good Sky

Acceptance of how our cultures and spiritual practices coexist in this world is one of the many things Dad, our Spiritual Adviser, helped us understand. Now, hardly anyone would blink twice if they saw Dad standing next to the preacher at a funeral.

Despite giving up the colleges when he became Spiritual Adviser, nothing really changed in his schedule. Dad continued to help everyone that he could. I thought his exhaustion would catch up to him, and on one particular night, it almost did.

He had gone to Tower to give someone medicine. He stayed with them late into the night until he knew they would be okay. Around 3:00 a.m., in the pitch black of early morning, he started the long drive home. There was no moon that night, and the narrow roads felt darker than normal. Without any snow on the ground or the moon to light the path, Dad struggled to focus on driving.

He'd driven that road hundreds of times before, but between the dark night and the late hour, he felt his head drooping. He jerked awake as the car crossed over the white lines. He shook his head, trying to rid the sleep that was calling him. And then he felt something to his left. He turned his head and saw the tiny dancing, white lights. The same lights he had seen surround both Rose and Gahmaht when they were with the medicine man.

He immediately felt awake as the lights danced in front of the car, allowing him to remain focused. They stayed with him until he turned onto the Reservation Road. He arrived home safely and grateful for being sent the help for the trip home.

I know he continued to push himself, despite my concern. But his life is marked, you know, by those coincidences that are far from coincidence. And he was also protected. That much was clear.

There were times I wondered how he managed, even after this point, to continue pouring so much of himself into the community. But he is a Warrior, and I suppose he never really left the service. He simply learned who it was he was called to serve.

Dianna Good Sky

20

THE WARRIOR

W hat was happening in Nett Lake and the surrounding communities regarding the cultural growth through ceremonies, blessings, the drum circle, the medicine for the people, the teachings for the kids (of all ages), and the language was nothing short of remarkable.

One of the cultural practices that Dad included in his lessons at Nett Lake Elementary and Orr High School was the Pow Wow. The traditional dancing, the drumming, the spiritual practices had been subdued for so long. Even my siblings and I were mostly unfamiliar with these traditions.

Growing up, I remember the summer Pow Wow—the one my Grandma and Grandpa used to take me to—was small. By small, I mean, there were maybe three drums present, sometimes less, sometimes more. When I visited home in 1995 (my military duties prevented me from traveling home, easily, prior to my retirement that year) for the summer Pow Wow, things were different. I counted thirteen drums at our *Sah Gii Ba Gah* celebration in June.

There were also so many more dancers. Especially young ones, in traditional regalia.

There were more ceremonies, more spectators in the bleachers, and I could sense the joy. The joy of being together, as family, as a community. I was floored at what I saw and the difference between then and before, and I knew that my dad and his commitment to teaching our ways had a lot to do with what I was seeing. I committed to making it home as often as I could from that point on. A promise I keep to this day.

The gap between the Natives and the non-Natives has been disappearing, especially at the schools. Dad received a note, once, from a former student expressing her gratitude for the things he taught.

> I've always loved seeing you around and respected your dedication to your family, the students, and teaching us so much!...I remember most of the ceremonies in elementary...and how it wasn't just about you guys (Natives) showing us your traditions, but you ALWAYS invited us all down to join at the end. And I feel like it was specifically you that would invite us. I swear there was nothing cooler. It wasn't just like, "these are our traditions and they are too sacred for you..." It was, "These are our sacred traditions and yet we welcome you into them." Beautiful stuff. You were always encouraging the unity and love that we need, even today more than ever. We truly are one. *Mii Gwetch!*
>
> Ericka (Schultz) Iverson

The ceremonies grow in size each year, and more and more members of the Tribe participate. Auntie Ellen, too, became a cultural teacher, extending the traditional ways to the next generation. Auntie Alma taught the ricing and sugar maple tapping in Sugar Bush with Dad. Uncle Whiz also taught in the schools for a while. And that is just my family.

Beyond Nett Lake, Native culture was also re-emerging as more and more people learned the old ways. What generations of laws, prejudice, and racism sought to destroy was coming back to life all around us.

I watched my family embrace their heritage, and I felt very proud of who I was, and where I fit in. The culture that I could not embrace for so long was starting to become *my* culture.

I watched Dad sing on the drum, and as time passed, my brother joined him. Today, my heart fills with joy as I listen to their beautiful voices, joined by Uncle Whiz and his own son, Leon.

Eventually, more cousins joined in on the drumming and singing. My sister learned to dance as a women's fancy shawl dancer. I watched her one year, her feet touching ever so lightly as she mimicked the movements of a butterfly. It was nothing like the sleep-deprived movements we made as children, spurred on by angry, drunken commands. My brother's dance movements were also so strong and powerful as he danced in his traditional men's regalia made by Mom and Grandma Gamaht.

The Nett Lake Summer Pow Wow, and those in the surrounding Tribes and communities, were growing every year as more and more Natives were finding their way back to traditions throughout Indian Country.

I retired from the Navy in 1995. By that time, I had fully embraced our culture and traditions too. My retirement ceremony was conducted with full Naval and Native American honors. It was a combined ceremony complete with the Commander in Chief Navy Band and a drum with Native American Singers. It was the first Native American retirement ceremony ever held.

The Tribe was gracious enough to fund the travel expenses so Dad, Gilbert Smith (and his drum), Uncle Whiz, and ten family members could attend as part of the ceremony. Dad did the opening and closing prayers in Anishinaabemowin while Uncle Whiz translated to English. It was amazing. What a strange thing, this life.

As I drove through the gate at Dam Neck Naval Base for my retirement ceremony, I saw a notice on the base billboard: "Welcome family and friends of OTAC Dianna Goodsky. Congratulations on your retirement." I couldn't help but remember that in 1980, my family had driven all the way down from Minnesota to attend my graduation from my Ocean Systems Tech School, only to be turned away from the base. I had been notified forty-five minutes before the ceremony that they would need a special sticker to be allowed on base. I don't remember other families or graduates having that same issue. What a difference fifteen years makes.

While Dad did not see me off to join the Navy, he was there to see me complete my Navy career and send me off in my new life as a civilian. A Native civilian. I am forever grateful. While at my retirement ceremony, Dad presented me with the highest honor a Native can receive: a white eagle feather.

Bringing a culture back from near extinction takes time. I know this well, because I am living it. As we slowly learn and come to terms with our culture, there is still work to do. Change is gradual.

Dad had a dream several years ago about the importance of our Indian names—naming is a significant part of our culture. My two middle children, Curtis and Nikole, received their Indian names as teenagers, around the time I was learning more about our ways. My youngest received hers when she was still in diapers. My oldest son, however, was born when I was just a teen. He still does not have an Indian name, and he is not alone. There are many others who grew up without the traditional ways.

At the time, Dad was already holding ceremonies for both Natives and non-Natives, including those who were unfamiliar with the Ojibwe traditions. Many of the people he served did not have Indian names.

In his dream, two spirits came to him—faceless and luminescent, like in past spiritual encounters. They spoke to him,

Dianna Good Sky

but only in his thoughts. They had no mouths from which to speak. They told him that they were glad he was serving all people, but because they were guided by people's names, they needed his help in order to be guided to those without Indian names.

They told Dad to get a white ribbon and cut it in two-inch pieces. When he performed a ceremony or prayer for anyone who lacked an Indian name, he was to fold a piece of ribbon in a circle and pin it to their clothing. "Tell them to wear it until the prayer or request has been answered," the spirits said. "This way, we will always be able to find them." Dad uses those ribbons even today, helping bridge the gap between the old ways and the new, the Natives and the non-Natives.

Our family has changed. When we're in the Village, we no longer try to hide from Dad. As a matter of fact, along with our newest little brother, Tom (Dad's bonus baby with Dorothea), we are always trying to get together. We grew up close with my mom's side of the family, but it took many years for us to be able to embrace Dad. It is so different from the days of hiding from him under the bed.

We have all changed regarding our culture as well. My brother is a singer and a Men's Traditional dancer. My sister is a fancy shawl dancer, and I am both a jingle dress and a traditional women's dancer.

In 1980, nothing could have prepared any of us for the dramatic change that would take place in all our lives on that cold, March night. Dad's sobriety, his commitment to walking the Red Road and living out the Creator's instructions—it changed us all. Our family is the biggest testament to not only Dad's experience, but the impact of his life.

Our children have grown up with a greater appreciation for and involvement in our culture than we ever had. My own bonus baby, Katherine, was brought in the Pow Wow circle as soon as she could walk, wearing a jingle dress made by me and my mom. My siblings and I all have our Indian names. We all practice our own ceremonies. We know where to go and what to do.

Learning the language has proven more difficult, so none of us are fluent. But we understand it much better than we used to. And personally, while I do wish that we could have learned Anishinaabemowin growing up, I no longer harbor resentment about why I do not know the language. Letting go and being more understanding of why my parents did what they did, came with time. It wasn't easy, but forgiveness usually isn't. It comes with opening your heart and mind: they couldn't do life any differently, because they didn't know anything different.

To say that I have forgiven Dad is to speak the truth. Dad has made amends on so many levels, that it is sometimes hard to remember the stinky drunk guy that I used to be afraid of. And frankly, there came a point in my life that I realized, if the Creator could forgive him, how can I not?

Dad retired from teaching after thirty-three years. I noticed a shift in him after he retired. He suddenly aged. I believe the students kept him young. He used to brag how he could keep up when running with the fifth graders during recess and loved challenging them to a race. Once he left the school system, his health took a turn.

He was the Spiritual Advisor for the tribe until just recently when the Tribal Council decided this position was no longer necessary. There is so much I want to say about this, but I will keep it short. This was a mistake.

As far as Dad is concerned, he remains available to those who need his help. He continues to do all that he can to help anyone who asks. If you're looking for him, he's likely driving around town dropping off diapers to a mom who ran out of money or dropping off medicinal tea. He'll drive to any one of the local towns to pick someone up when their car breaks down. He's even

Dianna Good Sky

been known to go as far away as Duluth or Minneapolis. Or he'll meet someone at the bank to give them money to feed their family. When he can, he loves stopping at Pattenn's Café in Orr for food or a visit with old friends.

He attends most of the high school sporting events. His loud cheer defies his aging, weakening body. The athletes will tell you that he is their most loyal and consistent fan.

You'll see Dad in hospitals visiting the sick and the dying. Most of the local hospitals know him and they understand that he is there for ceremony and prayer. They call him by his first name and most often, he is greeted with a smile.

He lost count of the number of people who called upon him as they contemplated suicide, and he helped them through their dark moments.

He conducts special ceremonies for healing, both with his drum and with his pipe, much like he did for Ryan Holman. Remember Ryan? He went on to become a very successful businessman. He owns and operates Ryan's Rustic Railings between Cook and Orr. Russell still operates his business, Voyageur Homes in Orr. Dad, Ryan, and Russ are great friends to this day.

One of Dad's favorite stories is about the day Ryan approached him, a few years after his accident, and asked him to come to his shop. He told Dad to bring his truck. When Dad arrived, Ryan gifted him with the most beautiful handmade log table. Dad cherishes that table and told me I could have it after he's gone (sorry siblings).

After being in charge of the Pow Wow committee for years, Dad has stepped down from that role as well, but he still participates as the head dude in charge. And he wouldn't miss an opportunity to sit and sing at the drum.

It has been a long road, and his favorite place to be is Sugar Bush, fishing on his dock. He lives there now, in a three-bedroom trailer. That is where his heart is. It is in Sugar Bush that he is connected to all who came before him. His brother—Uncle Whiz—lives there, too.

Warrior Spirit Rising

Sugar Bush has changed as much as the rest of us. It is where we connect as a family and, sometimes, as a community. When I drive up the dirt road, surrounded by beautiful trees, and get out of my car, it's as if I can feel the blanket of love being draped around my shoulders. It is like that for all of us, now.

It is where we fish, where we boat and barbeque, where we sing, where we see Richardson's Shangri-La Resort in all its glory across the bay. It is where Dad still makes canoe paddles for ricing, where he brews his teas, where he repairs the drums and blesses them before use in the Pow Wow. He collects most of his plants here, and it's where he watches Satellite Television, and every morning, records the outside temperature and his glucose readings before he starts his day.

Sugar Bush is where Dad smokes his pipe when someone's sister is sick in the hospital and they need guidance. Usually, after the ceremony, he will invite them in to join him for breakfast. Often, they will get a call during breakfast that the patient Dad just prayed for is doing better.

This healing gift, that started so long ago—the day he picked up the charcoal offered by his grandfather—remains one of his most treasured gifts.

Dad carries many gifts. He is a healer, teacher, counselor, and guide. He is a drummer and singer, and he is a Warrior. But his greatest gift came the night he nearly died, the night he met the Creator. He still calls it a dream. I think his life tells a different story.

That night, Dad received the gift of love. That overwhelming sense of love that births forgiveness and faith. To truly forgive is divine, and that night marked the beginning of Dad's journey into forgiveness. He first had to forgive himself, love himself, before he could pass that on to others. And he did. His life—our lives—are a testament to that. This is his greatest gift.

While there was a bit of time that I wanted to believe that Dad sobered up because he told me he would, I now know he was touched by the Great Spirit, and it had nothing to do with me.

Dianna Good Sky

Dad was sent back to help others, to accomplish the work set in front of him. His job has been done so very well, both for his people, our people, and for many others.

His memory is fading, and he sometimes gets confused as he recalls stories, but we are here to help him with that. And to carry on.

He awoke the Warrior in all of us.

Dad, your blue-eyed daughter loves you.

MiiGwetch. Thank you.

EPILOGUE

T his one particular old medicine man used to call me Na Ga Mo Dah, *which means 'Let's sing.'"*

Dad's voice floated across the room in what I can only describe as a soothing, Native cadence. I marveled at the difference in his voice, once gruff and stern. Now I find it calming. We were sitting together in Sugar Bush, talking about his story, about this book. As he talked, I experienced something profound: a deeper understanding of the calling he received so long ago and what that has meant in his life and the lives of so many others. He continued his story.

At that time, the reason he called me that is because I had a dream about a drum sitting in the middle of the field, right by my Auntie Jessie Drift, by her house.

In my dream, there were a bunch of people just laying around.

Some were on their elbows, some were sitting up, but the majority of them were just laying around. I could tell that they didn't look right or feel right. Something was just not right with them, laying around in that field.

So, I got up and I walked over to the drum that was sitting by itself in the middle of that field.

I sat down.

I picked up a stick, and I hit the drum.

I hit the drum four times. I didn't know, that's just what they usually do.

And I started singing. (And I never sang before.)

This was in my dream.

And pretty soon, people started sitting up. Some of the guys came over to the drum and they started pounding the drum with me and they started singing, and pretty soon, the rest of the people started getting up.

They started dancing around the drum.

And then I woke up.

Dianna: When was this, Dad?

Dad: It was after I had come back from the Navy, when I got out of the service.

Dianna: Were you still drinking then, when you had that dream? Or was it after you got sober? Do you have any idea how long after?

Dad: Probably a few years, I quit drinking in 1980, and after that is when I started helping this medicine man.

Dianna: What was the medicine man's name?

Dad: William Benner, his English name. But everybody called him Nassi. And that's why he used to call me Na Ga Mo Dah, because by that time, me and my brother and a couple other people started practicing singing. We used an old bass drum. Then eventually we got to increase our number of songs we were singing. After about a year, we were able to bring the drum to the Pow Wow.

The drum is a significant symbol within the Native American community and within our Tribe and family. There are so many types of drums: the drums of the Pow Wow that call us to dance.

Warrior Spirit Rising

War drums. Healing drums. Water drums that are nearly lost to history.

This drum that Dad dreamt of was the drum of a Warrior.

After his experience—the one that brought him back to life—Dad continued to have many spiritual messages. This dream, however, would end up being the guiding force behind his life, behind his mission to bring change and cultural revival.

In many ways, the drum is symbolic of Native American culture as a whole. It causes people to move. The vibrations of its beat compel us to action, and even speak to our souls.

Dad's drum—the heartbeat of his very life—is the call of the Warrior spirit, encouraging those around him to come awake, come alive. He carries this message in everything he does. This beat invokes our spirits to rise, as well. And so, we do.

Dianna Good Sky

AUTHOR'S NOTE

While I was sitting at Dad's table in Sugar Bush, gathering his stories, I asked him if he could offer people traditional Ojibwe advice on how to live. I knew basic concepts, such as be kind, be respectful, and honor your elders, but not much more. Dad surprised me with his answer. He pointed to an eagle feather on the wall above his table and told me that our life is like "that feather."

When we are born, he said, the shaft is strong. As we grow older, the shaft gets thinner. Sometimes, this means that it is harder to stay on the right path.

I immediately pictured a red line down the shaft of the feather. This is our road. We live our best life when we stay on that Red Road. Where the shaft meets the vanes is where our human life begins. Each vane represents a different path—a path we are not supposed to take, even though it could be very tempting. Some paths are fun, but really not in our best interest.

Dad went on to say that every time we stray from the shaft, we get off balance.

But of course! I thought. *Each vane represents a deviation from our Red Road—our purpose, our joy, our happiness.*

Then he said, "Each diversion, ranging from bad behavior when we're young, to being disrespectful, to lying, stealing, cheating, partying, being mean...each time you stray, you can come back. But you have to decide to go back." He watched me, his dark eyes inviting me to learn and understand.

"And if you haven't strayed too far," he continued, "it's kind of easy to get back on the right track. But sometimes if you stray far, like, say alcoholism, and you fall off. When you fall off the feather, you can never get back on your path by yourself. That is when you need help. You need others to help you. You need faith. You have to *believe*," he said loudly, "that you can get back on, and with the help of others, you can."

As I stared at that eagle feather, I knew that it was a perfect representation of the advice I was wanting to share with others on how to live our lives in this human existence.

The choices we make need to be in alignment with who we are. If we stray, we must choose to get back. Some of the paths, the vanes, are easy to return from; some are not. Some of the vanes are thick and easy to traverse, while others are so thin that it's easy to fall off.

Each deviation off of our path is a lesson that we learn as we walk through life. When we refuse to learn from our missteps, these lessons are presented again and again until we get it right— until we choose to stay on our Red Road. By the time we near the end of our journey in this life, we gain the wisdom needed to do better and our missteps and lessons become shorter and less arduous, like the vanes at the tip of the feather. We simply learn to make better choices.

This was reflected so clearly in my dad's life—and even in my own. He fell off—far off—the Red Road. With help and spiritual guidance, he was able to get back on the right path.

It was because of this conversation with my dad that I chose to include the red line down the feather on the cover of this book.

Dianna Good Sky

We are all walking on the Red Road, regardless of our history, our race, our culture, or our nationality. We are all walking the path of self-discovery.

So, I leave you with this: Stay on the straight and narrow Red Road on the feather of your life. It holds great promise for you if you believe.